Contents

Virtual Learning and Higher Education

Virtual Learning and Higher Education

Edited by

David Seth Preston

Amsterdam – New York, NY 2004

The paper on which this book is printed meets the requirements of "ISO 9706:1994, Information and documentation – Paper of documents – Requirements for permanence".

ISBN: 90-420-1129-7
©Editions Rodopi B.V., Amsterdam – New York, NY 2004
Printed in The Netherlands

Welcome to an *At the Interface* Project

At the Interface is a series of 3-5 day annual marquee conference projects designed specifically to challenge and explore subjects which cross the boundaries of individual disciplines, subject areas, professions and vocations. Deliberately designed to have a wide remit, they take a broad sampling of issues from within a subject area in order to lay the foundations for future development and take a snap-shot of where the key issues lie.

Conferences organised under the banner of *At the Interface* seek to promote truly inter- and multi-disciplinary dialogue and enable genuinely creative thinking across a wide range of areas. These conferences invite people working within academia, government, NGO's, charities, industry, business, vocations and other areas to share their perspectives as part of the dialogue.

Virtual Learning and Higher Education is part of the *Higher Education* portfolio of research projects. Higher education institutions have been criticized for living in the past; some have even proclaimed that the University has lost it's relevance. In the midst of these analyses and criticisms, the advent of Information and Communication Technologies in today's universities/colleges is seen as a promising development. What future has Higher Education when the virtual world of on-line education has so much more to offer? The aim of this series will be to examine Virtuality within Higher Education in an attempt to critique both its essential characteristics and its future possibilities to influence the education of adult learners.

Dr Robert Fisher
Inter-Disciplinary.Net
http://www.inter-disciplinary.net

Preface

This book began as one of the main products of a conference entitled 'Virtual Learning and Higher Education' held at Mansfield College (Oxford) in September 2002. The conference led to much discussion, mostly carried out, appropriately, via the Internet, to which both original conference delegates and others contributed. As a result of these 'chats' it became clear that the Internet affords a significant challenge to Higher Education (HE) and it is far from clear how the sector would be best advised to respond.

In selecting the chapters for this book I have tried to preserve some of the diversity of opinion presented at Oxford. Despite this diversity however, there is a consensus among many individual contributors, including myself, in seeing both the tremendous potential modern information technology affords and the many potential pitfalls it harbours. I have tried to preserve the philosophical nature of this *At the Interface* series by including only chapters that deal in some way with an issue or problem that 'Virtual Learning' affords. Papers that described simply how to create such 'spaces' were rejected outright. Perhaps it was Mark Stiles' contribution that surprised me most revealing as it does his split persona. Here is an educator who has designed and constructed one of the most extensive and user-friendly of virtual learning tools, COSE and yet here too is man who has clearly defined issues with the use of such tools both for now and in the future.

The book is divided into three main parts with the chapters arranged in a 4-3-3 formation: 'Frontierland: Exploring the Uses of Virtual Learning Environments in Higher Education'; 'Into the Unknown: Charting the Future of Virtual Learning Environments in Higher Education'; and 'Looking Before Leaping: Issues in Virtual Higher Education'.

In Chapter One, Kate Boardman and Mike Waring outline and explore the use and potential of a Virtual Learning Environment (VLE) developed to improve access to reflective practice and a researching pedagogy in the development of physical education trainee teachers and their mentors as part of a predominantly school-based one year Post-Graduate Certificate in Education course of initial teacher training .

In Chapter Two, Melissa Lee Price and Andy Lapham examine how mode of study, course of study, and previous educational background relate to students' perceptions of the distance learning experience. Results show that students who were re-entering higher education after a number of years adapted to the 'any time, any place' of asynchronous teaching with a higher level of satisfaction than 'traditional' students. Traditional students also wanted more synchronous online meetings and felt more isolated during the learning experience. The non-traditional students were intimidated by the educational experiences of the traditional students and the traditional students were intimidated by the work experience of the non-traditional students. The computer-mediated environment allowed both groups the opportunity to have their voice heard and to ease the feelings of intimidation.

In Chapter Three, Alan David and Lynda Ross consider a new Strategic University Plan (SUP) within a Canadian university. Integral to the SUP was a commitment to the use of technology to improve access and to remove barriers to learning and a significant expansion of online infrastructures to support e-learning throughout North America. In concert with the SUP, the E-Learning Plan (ELP) was created to provide direction for the development of e-learning. The strategies used and the challenges faced are the subjects of this chapter.

In Chapter Four, Brent Muirhead shows how contemporary Internet technologies are helping remove the idea of distance from online education. The online teaching and learning process could produce more relevant and consistent interaction than currently available in traditional classrooms. Dr. Muirhead examines how the Internet is providing a practical way to remove learning barriers and to encourage greater access to intellectual resources. He suggests that the idea of distance education has fostered the pursuit of new educational paradigms that encourage online education to be more personal and student-centred.

In Chapter Five, Craig Thomson suggests Information and Communications Technologies (ICT) are central to the lifelong learning policy in the UK. He argues that whilst policy has resulted in significant spending on new infrastructure, insufficient attention is being paid to the ways in which those in the workplace learn and learn about learning. Dr. Thomson believes radical changes in the way that work-based learning is conceptualised and organised are needed. The chapter explores the potential for new learning relationships to be recognised and taken fully into account in planning and implementing work-based learning programmes.

In Chapter Six, Mark Stiles argues the necessity of institutional strategies to overtly address the professional development of staff in the dual contexts of the educational needs of widening participation and inclusion and the pedagogic challenges these bring. The chapter argues that 'traditional' models of teaching and learning as practised in higher education may well be inadequate for the 'new' higher education and makes claims for the need for the immediate adoption of active pedagogies which may well be unfamiliar to many academics. In addition, the author considers the pressures on both HE and Further Education (FE) sectors to adopt the use of Managed and Virtual Learning Environments (MLEs and VLEs). These pressures have led to the adoption of systems which seriously underestimate the pedagogic challenges and which may lead to the business and educational processes of institutions becoming constrained by their adopted technologies. It is argued that given the evidence of earlier failures in learning technology to produce sustainable impact on practice, the cumulative effect of the problems and pressures discussed may lead to the current round of e-learning systems being very short-lived.

In Chapter Seven, Mike Fuller examines the use of tests which are a common feature of VLEs. The chapter reviews the use of VLEs for assessment. The conclusion is that while there are inherent limitations in the specific assessment tools of a VLE, there is great potential for use in a variety of developmental assessment contexts. Consideration of the potential scope of VLEs in assessment raises some questions about Bloom's taxonomy of the cognitive domain which Dr. Fuller investigates.

In Chapter Eight, James Wood revisits C.P.Snow's warning that the gulf between two academic cultures was getting so wide to be to the detriment of public interest. The two cultures he described were those of the "literary intellectuals" and the scientists. Today there is a similar gulf, but this time between the faculty and the university administration. It is argued in this chapter that whilst faculty has maintained a commitment to outstanding teaching and scholarship, the university administration has increasingly devised strategic plans for the university that stress other goals: the business model in general and the financial bottom-line in particular.

In Chapter Nine, Adrian Bromage considers the ontological basis of synchronous learning in multi-user Virtual Reality (VR) systems, how this might compare to that in the physical world and with what practical consequences. It is suggested that the essential features of synchronous learning communities can be reproduced in virtual reality, including a genuine feeling of community, though this is with less emotional solidarity between participants and with novel behaviour enabled by the technology. Dr. Bromage suggests there are significant implications for online learning and examines these through some work carried out at Coventry University.

My own contribution is Chapter Ten where I examine how throughout history the University has tried various approaches to the challenge of technology. Oxbridge tried to ignore it for over a hundred years. Others have greeted technology with open arms. Increasingly, ICTs dominate university concerns for the future. Terms such as 'e-learning' and 'virtual university' are constantly discussed and considered even in the most conservative of universities. Some see it as a new light that will bring radiance to the university, others as a permanent storm. My chapter considers whether or not such technologies are a threat to the university and whether they can realise the claims made on their behalf.. In addition, I examine the values that often accompany such technocratic vision.

I am grateful to all the contributors and the Series Editor Rob Fisher for their valiant effort in meeting most of my deadlines and responding to my endless e-mails with remarkable enthusiasm and speed. It has been a remarkably painless and enjoyable experience working with you all. In addition, I owe an enormous debt to Andrew Bartlett for his brilliance in formatting, editing, proofreading and all manner of technological talents.

As ever, I am extremely fortunate in having a wonderful family and it is them to whom this book is dedicated.

For
Margaret, Benjamin, Rachel and Gabriella

Dr D.S. Preston
London
Email: David-Preston@blueyonder.co.uk

Part I

Frontierland: Exploring the Uses of Virtual Learning Environments in Higher Education

Learning to Teach, Teaching to Learn:
A Developmental Framework for Teacher Training

Mike Waring and Kate Boardman

Abstract

The purpose of this chapter is to outline and explore the use and potential of a virtual learning environment (VLE) developed to support trainee teachers and their mentors in a predominantly school-based one year physical education (PE) Post Graduate Certificate in Education (PGCE) course of initial teacher training (ITT) in an English University. The aim of the VLE was to enhance access to reflective practice and a researching pedagogy.

1. Introduction

As Curran and Foster independently have pointed out in recent years there have been many new technologies and e-activities that have been hailed as agents of educational transformation (Curran, 2001; Foster, 2001). And yet education - or at least formal education as practised in schools and colleges - has remained stubbornly resistant to change (Curran, 2001, 113). Perhaps there is no better place to begin the change than with trainee teachers and their mentors in schools. This chapter describes the experiences gained from the implementation and use of Durham University Online (duo) by PE PCGE trainees and mentors in the 2000/2001 academic year.

We believe, along with Furlong, that higher education (HE) has a unique contribution to make to the realisation of a new teaching profession, and it is "the ability of those in HE to work with teachers and other professional to help them engage with 'practical theory'" (Furlong, 2000, 3). Hawkridge states that there are four principal rationales for introducing technology: social; vocational; catalytic; and pedagogical (Hawkridge et al, 1990). At this point it is worth noting that the overriding reason for the development of the VLE described here was predominantly that it was seen as an innovation that would be pedagogically more effective and a means to promote real and efficient change in education. However, one cannot escape from the perception of most trainees (and mentors/teachers) that the bottom-line motivation for most initiatives is assessment. In the case of the trainee teachers and their mentors this relates to the achievement of the Standards for Qualified Teacher Status (QTS) (DfES/Teacher Training Agency, 2002).

The shift from a predominantly university-based to a school-based teacher training programme has to an extent altered the nature of the interaction between the tutor and trainees. However, the nature of the accountability in essence has not changed; it fundamentally remains with the university (Alpin, 2001). Face-to-face contact time between student and tutor has been very much reduced with trainees more heavily reliant upon their relationship with one or more mentors in school. One of the challenges facing university tutors is that of ensuring clear and productive lines of communication between the three parties in order to monitor and enhance the trainees' and mentors' learning as well as that of the pupils. The sharing of documentation and keeping of records accessible by students, mentors and tutors must also be carefully managed.

School-based teacher training provides for considerable experiential learning in the classroom. However, it is essential that the trainees maintain a broader viewpoint, that they have opportunities to: reflect on their teaching practice, both individually and with their peers; extend their understanding of the relationship between their classroom activities and accepted and developing pedagogy; to continue their studies of legislation, guidelines, theory and practice in education; and to explore and follow up new developments or resources in their chosen specialist subjects.

As part of the ITT National Curriculum for the use of ICT in subject teaching all trainees have to be able to exploit the potential of ICT to meet their teaching objectives (DfES/Teacher Training Agency, 2002). Therefore, ITT providers must equip trainees to demonstrate that "they know how to use ICT...effectively, both to teach their subject and to support their wider professional role" (DfES/Teacher Training Agency, 2002, 8). However, despite the compulsory nature of its inclusion in the ITT curriculum in England, the use of any technology has to be considered on the basis of its significance and integrity to the teaching/learning of the individual in a given context rather than merely an end in itself. The PE VLE therefore has to ensure that the trainees' appreciate the broader picture associated with policy and implementation and their present and evolving place in that context relative both to their personal understanding and competence of ICT hardware and software and to the specific school context and children they are teaching.

Other considerations, all of which are important in the preparation of trainees, also have to be acknowledged as they too will impact on the structure and content of the VLE. Significantly, these considerations do not exist independently of each other, reinforcing the need to cross-reference the learning tasks and material from all contexts. As part of the general paradigm shift from a behaviourist to a constructivist framework, the knowledge taught in schools and universities needs to be retrievable in real-life, using problem-solving contexts and highlighting the interdependence of situation and cognition (Herrington and Oliver, 2000;

Mayes, 2001). Such cross-referencing can be facilitated through the VLE. Limited application of subject specific knowledge has been considered by Her Majesty's Inspectors (HMI) and others as an issue in the training of Physical Education PGCE trainees as they work to translate their knowledge base and delivery, usually from a predominantly coaching to a predominantly teaching orientation. Once again, the nature of technology employed in the teaching and learning of the subject (PE in this case) must ensure not only that the trainee is aware of the potential of a variety of sources of stimuli and information for themselves and for pupils but, importantly, that they exploit it in their teaching of their subject. This creates a potential problem in that, as with the level of subject knowledge, there are a number of levels of competence (as a performer and academic) with which the trainees can arrive, despite application of stringent recruitment standards (academic and practical). The issue therefore becomes one of auditing and differentiating the learning experience of each trainee and the monitoring of each trainee's progress relative to the Standards for QTS. Consequently there is the need for constant and consistent formative and summative assessment in a variety of forms throughout the life of a programme. This raises the need for pro-active communication and robust quality assurance and improvement procedures including quality mentoring.

It is essential that if a baseline measure of standards is to be achieved and then developed there has to be a reliable mechanism of communication that involves all the key agents: the university, the school and the trainee. Each of them must be able and allowed to question, enquire and comment upon every aspect of the programme and their progress relative to the Standards for QTS, so that in a sense of real partnership the trainee, the mentor and the university tutor can cater for the changing needs of the individual trainee as and when appropriate.

If this kind of partnership is to be fully realised then the provision and development of quality mentoring, and a consistent provision of school-based training involving the translation of the progressive generalised learning activities provided by the university into more differentiated ones for each trainee (and mentor) have to be achieved (Waring, 2002a). Associated with this is the access trainees and mentors have to appropriate resources in the school when teaching. Quality mentoring is not solely associated with the communication network but also with the nature of the information that outlines and defines the expectations of everyone involved.

There must be excellent documentation in a variety of forms (hard copy and electronic) to ensure that objectives, learning outcomes and standards are clearly established for each segment of the programme and that they are cross-referenced with associated elements. Trainees and mentors then have the fundamental framework for an overall picture of their development as learners and teachers of PE. This way they will be in a more informed position to appreciate and manipulate those essential pedagogical principles (and the necessary content) which permeate the teaching of their subject.

The interrelated nature of each of these issues, as well as the many other associations which have not been identified here, creates a very daunting task if they are to be addressed in a VLE. The VLE to which the group of trainees have been exposed is Durham University Online (duo), implemented by the University of Durham's Learning Technologies Team in August 2000. A VLE is an integrated solution to manage online learning and improve student learning. VLEs offer not only facilities to structure learning content but also provide student management, communication and assessment tools and a range of other useful functions.

A VLE usually consists of course details and objectives, lecture notes/summaries, reading lists, learning resources and (Computer-Assisted Learning) CAL materials, discussion groups and assessment. While tutors may have a similar physical view of the learning environment to students, they do have additional tools and privileges that allow them to add materials, create conferences and track students' progress. The flexibility of a VLE enables tutors to support different learning and teaching styles. For most campus-based undergraduate programmes, the provision of a VLE allows an enhancement of standard teaching methods and the easy delivery of extra resources. The extended benefits of a VLE for off-campus programmes are potentially much more widespread. The extended benefits (principally in improved communication) of a VLE for off-campus programmes made the PE PGCE course, in which trainees spend two-thirds of their training year in a school setting rather than the university, an ideal candidate for inclusion in the pilot of duo.

2.   Physical Education PGCE Virtual Learning Environment

The trainee teachers arrive at the beginning of the PE PGCE course with the expectation that it will be intensive in terms of time commitment and workload. However, despite rigorous interview procedures and high calibre experienced trainees, they still (and quite understandably) are taken aback by the amount and intensity of work. They have to makes shifts in their approach and manipulate their subject knowledge and its application to consistently establish effective learning environments for pupils in a school context. Consequently, in order to facilitate this 'developmental shift process' trainees have to be allowed, in a user-friendly manner, to navigate their way through all of the documentation and information (administrative and subject related) with which they are bombarded at the beginning of and throughout the course

(Waring, 2002b). It is worth noting that despite the fact that all of the trainees have an upper second class honours degree or above, their experience and application of ICT was variable. Therefore, it was essential to develop a structure and a framework that was both systematic and regimented but at the same time flexible enough to allow trainees to explore and develop at different rates above a minimum expectation. Consequently the PE PGCE VLE was built around eight interrelated 'zones'.

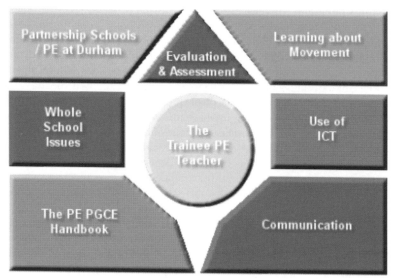

Figure 1. The PE PGCE VLE Schematic

A. Partnership Schools

This zone provides information about all the schools involved in the delivery of the PE PGCE programme including photographs, names and addresses of mentors, contact and website details of schools and links to their OFSTED reports. In addition to this, there is an area within duo for mentors to communicate with each other, entering into discussion and sharing good practice.

B. Evaluation and Assessment

This is a zone that contains information on the formative and summative assessments associated with the PE PGCE course. Students, tutors and mentors have access through this section to compulsory proformas such as Profiles of Achievement, ICT, Subject and Pedagogical Knowledge Audit Booklets in an online format. From such a baseline of information this zone has great potential to utilise some of the features of the VLE such as the embedding of formative/diagnostic testing and review. These have so far been called school foci and study tasks. The school foci are mini-action research topics for the trainee and their mentor to collaboratively investigate. The study tasks relate more to the production and evaluation of resources. They are an attempt to get the trainee to develop their subject knowledge and their appreciation of pedagogical issues around the permeating theme or activity area.

C. Learning about Movement

This was intended to be an ever-evolving zone designed to provide a repository of digital data, diagrams, photographs and a collection of digital video/stills and scanned images each accompanied by evolving reflective commentaries from staff and students. The idea behind this is that critical features and key principles could be highlighted and with guidance on how these can be best translated into different learning environments. This also incorporates reference to literature and links to online and offline resources. The intention of such a design is to enhance and encourage a continued learning process about the essence of movement and the context of the activity areas of the school PE National Curriculum.

D.   Whole School Issues (WSI)

This zone provides access to keynote lectures and material common to all PGCE trainees and mentors, regardless of specialist subject. This allows trainees, who spend a significant part of their time in schools, to have access to the core documentation 24 hours per day. This includes options for them to explore additional material related to the generic issues that permeate the whole range of curriculum subjects in the PGCE programme. The PE programme and the WSI programme are cross-referenced on a content and chronological basis to ensure maximum reinforcement and progression.

E.   Use of ICT

This is a large zone that provides links to a wealth of online resources in this area including a wide range of sporting and educational websites and e-journals. These provide a permanent resource for trainees to access and develop both their content knowledge and pedagogical understanding. This is constantly updated and revised by trainees who can submit new resources and venues to be included at any time and can be accessed from any PC connected to the Internet.

F. The PGCE Handbook

This zone contains all the information in the PE PGCE Course Handbook such as the course objectives, the objectives and content and reading for every lecture, the particular standards for QTS, performance expectations, and a 'school focus' (a school-based task) associated with each session, as well as assessments and a list of all of the required standards for QTS. Access to the PowerPoint presentations and extension materials for each lecture is also included.

G. Communication

This is a fundamental component of the online PGCE PE course. One of the major concerns of the university tutor dealing with predominantly school-based trainees is that of maintenance of regular effective communication. When contact time at university may on occasions be as little as one day per week for subject studies, communication via the VLE is considered a priority. Significantly, not only is there potentially reduced communication between trainees and tutor during block teaching placements in school but it can also be difficult for the trainees themselves to bond with their peers. This is something that can inhibit a very important and effective support and development mechanism for the trainees. The social dimension of the VLE is very powerful and should not be, but unfortunately has been, either ignored or deemed superficial in many academic environments. Despite school visits and the maintenance by students of a journal that is discussed weekly with their mentors, there was a strong desire by all agents to enhance interaction between trainees, tutors and mentors. Hence, this was considered to be the first priority for the online course to address. With the facility for synchronous and asynchronous communication through email, discussion groups and virtual chat, the learning environment could meet this need from the day the students began their programme of study at Durham University.

H. The Trainee PE Teacher

The concept of the trainee PE teacher as an individual underpins the whole course and educational process. Consequently, this is reflected and reinforced by the central location on the schematic of the Trainee PE Teacher zone. This zone provides information on how to develop teaching and learning skills and ICT competence. The zone additionally shows how to create a personal web page and online CV as a testament to the trainee's development throughout the course and beyond in relation to interviews and professional development.

3.   Getting the Process Started

An introductory session to the learning environment was held during the induction week. Emphasis was placed on the practicalities of using duo to keep in touch with each other when they were in the University and in preparation for when the trainees would be distributed amongst their placement schools. The trainees began using the communication elements of duo immediately; as post-graduates, a significant majority lived out of university-run accommodation - some at quite a distance - and the chat room soon became a popular place for social and occasionally educational conversations. Discussion groups were run throughout the year on different topics around pedagogy and content and these have ranged from initial 'coffee shop' introductory forums to literature reviews and more in-depth evaluations of school-based, university-based and outdoor and adventure activities. The learning environment has presented this group of trainees with an opportunity to bond and collaborate as colleagues to an extent that was unavailable to previous cohorts who were not able to use the VLE.

Trainee teachers are inundated with documentation during their PGCE year (a taste of things to come in their teaching career), from lengthy explanations of required standards and submission proformas related to the university-based portion of the course, through a detailed journal kept throughout their university and school-based training, monitored and critiqued by both their school mentors and university tutor, to the comprehensive curriculum documents. The online PGCE course attempts to minimise confusion with explanations of the various forms of paperwork, examples of correctly completed documents, and the facility, where appropriate, for electronic submission. Maintenance of an electronic version of the PE Mentor Journal allows both mentors' and tutors' views to be recorded in addition to the trainees' views. Feedback may be offered at any point, when requested or deemed necessary (by mentor or tutor), with minimal interruption to the trainees' schedules.

None of the eight zones that make up the online PGCE PE course are designed to stand alone; rather they form part of a whole and inform each other and the rest of the course. Although the use of ICT is a required competency in a trainee teacher, the online PGCE PE course is not used primarily to train the trainees in the use of ICT. The PE PGCE Course in duo forms merely a part of the whole learning experience for the trainee PE teachers even though it is a central mode of delivery and through its use technology skills were instinctively and sub-consciously improved. Through the use of the learning environment the trainees can increase their skills and confidence in using computers and the Internet; they learn to manipulate electronic data, word-process, use communication tools, edit graphics and create web pages for their own learning and to enhance the learning of the pupils they teach. The learning environment can and should be seen as an extra teaching and learning arena for the PE trainees to exploit, one without restriction of location or time of day, in which they can study alone and come together to discuss and reflect upon their experiences in the classroom (and socially). The interactive bibliography and library of web-links cover sites maintained by government and key educational organisations giving access to and guidance through various resources. Trainees are permitted and expected to add to and build upon this archive as they explore the Internet and critique the educational value and potential of the sites they find. The aims are to reinforce and extend certain of their classroom experiences and university tuition and to set classroom teaching practice into the wider pedagogical context of current policy and legislation (Penney and Waring, 2000; Ireson et al, 1999). Trainees are encouraged to broaden their perspectives and the mechanisms with which they explore and evaluate the resources available to them, maintaining and developing their contextual knowledge during their PGCE year and beyond (Nicholls, 1999).

4.   Issues and Challenges

While some issues and challenges were addressed with the creation of the VLE, others were highlighted and some arose as a result of its use. The issue of access remained an issue regardless of the fact that the PE VLE could be accessed via the Internet anywhere in the world. Access must be of a suitable quality. In the majority of placement schools the staff (either via departmental computers or central 'staff room' based computers) can access the Internet. However, the quality of such access in what is a demanding, time-scarce context of teaching was poor and generally antiquated with slow access machines that severely inhibited the manipulation of any kind of data via the VLE. Therefore, the quality of the technology available in schools has become an issue in certain cases. There are other challenges that can exacerbate such a situation. The question of each mentor's ability and willingness to engage with the VLE (significant variables here include their technical ability and pedagogical appreciation) and to share their work and practice with everyone, including those outside their immediate personal context of mentor, trainee, school and university tutor. The issue of ownership between a mentor and trainee of their experiences, interactions and work together takes on a personal dimension which can make it difficult for them to readily 'expose' it to their peers (other mentors and other trainees). Therefore, there has to be a mechanism that facilitates anonymity as much as is possible in order to allow for experiences to be readily shared. Significantly, the term 'sharing good practice' has not been used here as the PE VLE was designed to share all practice, good as well as indifferent or unsuccessful experiences, both of which can be learned from. The PE VLE is an excellent mechanism for anonymous posting and sharing in a general and differential basis. The archive that it also offers regarding past discussions and notices is invaluable in assisting such a process of dissemination and professional debate.

However, the nature of the subject of Physical Education has created certain problems. Ethical issues impeded the development of the Learning About Movement zone which could otherwise have been the most influential. There were problems concerning the use of images of children that were to be videoed as part of the lessons conducted by the trainees. The essence of the movement zone was to explore and observe movement (a fundamental component of the subject). However, in order to ensure the ongoing and progressive development of each individual trainee and the whole PE cohort, it required up-to-date images of their experiences to critique and comment on so that their pedagogical (and subject knowledge) could evolve. Gaining consent for the use of images from parents, schools, pupils and the University proved to be a minefield. The protracted nature of the process of ethical considerations meant that the necessary immediacy of feedback on recent observations and the like was impractical. While images of children, especially in a physical activity setting, continue to be significant personal and legal areas of concern for local education authorities, schools, parents and university ethics committees, this will remain an area of untapped potential in the PE VLE, despite the password protection on the PE VLE.

Allied to this portion of the debate over the manipulation of images and data concerning children is the use of personal digital assistants (PDAs) to enhance the teaching and learning of trainees and the learning of the pupils they teach. The use of PDAs is potentially a significant development in enhancing the assessment of trainees and the trainees' assessment of pupils. They provide a genuinely useable tool for the promotion of achievement through the accessing, sharing and recording of information in a practical and classroom context. The use of spreadsheets of information remains the most obvious outcome. However, the pupils' recording of their own movements in the context of a lesson and for them to then use these images to evaluate and critique performance and understanding would surely be a significant tool for promoting learning. Even though the technology is now reasonably mature, PDAs have not exploited the use of moving images to any great extent. However, they provide a very useful means of accessing reference material. The interface between the use of PDAs in the class context (school and university) and the VLE should be an area for future development.

The feedback from trainees has been extremely positive - they have acknowledged the usefulness of the structure of the PE VLE to assist navigation around the documentation and standards. However, the flexibility of the VLE in allowing their needs and contributions to be shared and considered is also appreciated. In discussions about duo, trainees have acknowledged the interrelated and reinforcing nature of the zones, school foci and study tasks. The communication zone has been particularly successful in that it has enhanced the differentiated contact that the tutor has had with the trainees throughout the PGCE course regardless of block school placements. This has enabled the university tutor to achieve more continuous monitoring and evaluation of trainees' learning with relatively minimal increased demands on their time. The differentiated nature of the feedback has also been increased, especially during the prolonged school-based experiences of the trainees. This supports Ravenscroft's interpretation of computer mediated communication (CMC) in that we "should not treat the computer as a mere conduit of discourse, but as a powerful mediational tool that can support and promote the development of higher mental processes by designing interfaces that structure discourse and dialogue in ways that stimulate, support and favour learning" (Ravenscroft, 2001, 150). The interrelated nature of the zones in the environment is significant and something that will continue to evolve and alongside the pro-active communication and robust quality assurance and improvement procedures, facilitate a researching pedagogy and appropriately differential levels of reflective practice and for each trainee.

Curran is surely correct when he says: "Notwithstanding the continuing debate with respect to the effect of media on learning, few would question that these new technologies can enhance the quality of education and widen access to educational opportunity" (Curran, 2001, 128). The development of the PE VLE (and otherss like it) have to involve all the stakeholders (schools, mentors, trainees, tutors and universities), coming to terms with not only the pedagogical challenges and changes but also those related to the development of the system in regard to personal and school and university contexts. The position of the teacher in the learning process is not at question here, rather it is the evolution of existing educational paradigms currently employed in universities and schools to engage the teacher more in their own learning as well as that of the pupils.

References

Alpin, R. (2001), 'The changing face of initial secondary teacher education in England (1984-1998)', in: Cheng, Y.C., Chow, K.W. and Tsui, K.T. (eds.) *New teacher education for the future: International perspectives..*

Hong Kong: Hong Kong Institute of Education and Kluwer Academic Publishers, 243-260.

Curren, C. (2001), 'The Phenomenon of On-line Learning', *European jouranal of education,* 36(1), 113-132.

Department for Education and Skills / Teacher Training Agency (2002), *Qualifying to teach: Professional standards for Qualified Teacher Status and requirements for initial teacher training.* London: Teacher Training Agency.

Foster, M. (2001), *E-policy guidelines for education: Best Internet practice for schools and colleges.* Norwich, England: Schoolmanager/The Stationary Office.

Hawkridge, D., Jaworski, J. and McMahon, H. (1990), *Computers in Third World schools: examples, experiences and issues.* London: MacMillan.

Herrington, J. and Oliver, R. (2000), 'An Instructional Design Framework for Authentic Learning Environments', *Educational technology research and development.* 48(3), 23-48.

Ireson, J., Mortimore, P. and Hallam, S. (1999), 'The common strands of pedagogy and their implications', in: Mortimore, P. (ed.) *Understanding pedagogy and its impact on learning.* London: Paul Chapman Publishing, 212-232.

Mayes, T. (2001), 'Learning technology and learning relationships', in: Stevenson, J. (ed.) *Teaching and learning online: Pedagogies for new technologies.* London: Kogan Page, 18-26.

Nicholls, G. (1999), 'Continual professional development', in: Nicholls, G. (ed.) *Learning to teach: A handbook for primary and secondary school teachers.* London: Kogan Page, 202-209.

Ravenscroft, A. (2001), 'Designing e-learning interactions in the 21st Century: Revisiting and rethinking the role of theory', *European journal of education: Research, development and policies.* 36(2) , 133-156.

Penney, D. and Waring, M. (2000), 'The absent agenda. Pedagogy and physical education', *Journal of sport pedagogy.* 6(1), 4-37.

Waring, M. (2002a), 'Creating a reflective and developmental experience for all PE trainees involved in school-based ITE. *12th Commonwealth International Sports Conference*, Manchester, England.

Waring, M. (2002b), 'Enhancing learning and teaching: Creating a developmental framework for teacher education. *1st International Conference on Virtual Learning in Higher Education*. Oxford University, England.

The Virtual Seminar

Melissa Lee Price and Andy Lapham

Abstract
    This chapter examines how mode of study, course of study, and previous educational background relate to students' perception of the distance learning experience. Results show that students who were re-entering higher education after a number of years adapted to the 'any time, any place' mode of asynchronous teaching with a higher level of satisfaction than traditional students. Traditional students also wanted more synchronous online meetings and felt more isolated during the learning experience. The non-traditional students were intimidated by the educational experiences of the traditional students and the traditional students were intimidated by the work experience of the non-traditional students. The computer-mediated environment allowed both groups the opportunity to have their voice heard and eased the feelings of intimidation.

1.   Introduction

    This chapter reports on a study to discover significant differences in attitude regarding a distance education module based on mode of study (full- or part-time); course of study; or gender. The students involved in the study were taking Technological Innovations, their first module on an MA course of study. This was the first distance education experience for all students. The module required students to: post to an asynchronous bulletin board (BBS); attend several synchronous chat sessions; write a twenty page annotated bibliography; write a personal essay about the different modes of communication/teaching during the semester; and to participate in a joint project with another student. The module was worth 30 credits out of the 180 needed for an MA. Approximately five months after the online class ended students were asked to complete a self-assessment questionnaire about their experiences in the online class.

    Education is a social process with people interacting with other people: the teacher interacts with the learner; the learner interacts with the teacher; and, just as importantly; the learner interacts with other learners. Because education has become a matter of mass education, the learner has been replaced by 'learners' in the educational exchange. In traditional distance education the teacher - learner interaction was paramount. With some degree of difficulty the learner could interact with the teacher via posted mail or telephone calls. This process was time consuming and often resulted in learner frustrations that were responsible for high drop-out rates among correspondence students. With the advent of multimedia technology in distance education, the quality of teacher-learner, learner-teacher and learner-learner relationships can approach that of the traditional classroom.

There are many different kinds of traditional classroom. The most familiar is the large lecture situation in which the instructor addresses a number of students. This teaching method is based on a teacher to learner flow of information. It is with difficulty that a student can ask a question and discussion or debate is nearly impossible. Many distance education practitioners wish to replicate the traditional classroom experience causing universities to spend large sums of money installing satellite communication facilities to allow students to attend classes without having to attend campus. Even with the advent of the World Wide Web (WWW or Web), universities are still seeking ways to mimic the on-campus experience. Much of this technology is being applied in a traditional way to facilitate a lecture-style teaching approach. Students might be viewing from a laptop but the nature of the educational experience is still based on the traditional, passive lecture structure.

On the other hand, the Socratic seminar also has a valued place in the educational experience. Students are more in charge of their learning experience in a seminar situation. The seminar/tutorial form of instruction requires the student to come to the learning space prepared to contribute to the discussion. The discussion is the learning experience. Students arrive at some decision about the content of the seminar based on the actual seminar experience.

There are two distinct kinds of distant educational system: synchronous and asynchronous. In a synchronous system the learner and teacher occupy the same virtual space at the same time. This could be a system that involves video and audio or it could even be a text-based system. No matter what form the communication/teaching process involves, the learner is receiving at the same time that the teacher is delivering. An asynchronous system allows the learner and the teacher to be separated in time and virtual space. The teacher prepares some form of instructional material at some point and the student accesses the material at a future time. The communication process is time and space independent. The most common form of asynchronous communication today is email.

The asynchronous nature of most Computer Mediated Communication (CMC) releases the user from the constraints of space and time. Kaye suggests that this allows students to organise their learning time around their everyday lives (Kaye, 1989). Hiltz and Turoff offer a similar argument and additionally suggest that the asynchronous nature of CMC extends the opportunity for education and training to sectors of the community that would otherwise be unable to find the time (Hiltz and Turoff, 1993). On the other hand, Acker, in an explication of what he calls the "time/place paradox", argues that technology, rather than freeing up our time, actually enslaves us by squeezing more into the hours of the day (Acker, 1994). This point is demonstrated by the following quote from a Technological Innovations student:

> "Within half an hour after posting my initial introduction I received a reply and several other students had posted their self-presentations. I had fun replying to the message, so much fun that I became distracted from my work and I quickly realised that my place of employment was not the right environment to be continuously checking and replying to new messages." (Student 11 – from Personal essay).

The asynchronous CMC environment gives participants time to reflect and the opportunity to form a more cogent response or contribution to a discussion. Participants are also freed of the constraint to take turns to contribute. This in itself can democratise the group and improve many of the problems associated with face-to-face group activity.

This research is supported by some of the comments students in Technological Innovations made on the study questionnaire (see section 3).

> "Question 3 rates highly because I feel that the online format of the module gave me the opportunity to digest, research, and formulate ideas. I also had the opportunity to contribute at times of the day when normal face to face contact would be impossible therefore giving me the opportunity to express myself in a way that I would not have had the opportunity to do had the discussions taken place in a classroom setting." (Student 6 – from Questionnaire).
> "Question 3 rates highly because I felt more at ease talking online than I would in a normal class environment. The online experience also gave me the time to think to respond to the responses and issues brought up." (Student 12 – from Questionnaire).

Feenberg describes the *communication anxiety* that occurs over the lack of an immediate response to a contribution to a CMC discussion (Feenberg, 1989). Hiltz and Turoff, on the other hand, argue that participants in synchronous modes of communication experience more anxiety over the lack of immediate responses to their contributions than participants in asynchronous modes of communication (Hiltz and Turoff, 1993). In this argument they suggest that expectations in a synchronous mode are akin to expectations in face-to-face communication whilst expectations in an asynchronous mode are more akin to those in letter writing and therefore no immediacy of response is expected. This apparent paradox of views can probably be explained by the fact that technological developments since Hiltz and Turoff originally published their text in 1978 have made CMC exchanges potentially rapid enough to be more like spoken conversation and less like letter writing.

> ".... Looking back on the notes that I made at the time it seems ridiculous that I hesitate [sic] so long before I posted the first message, and that I was unsure that I had completed the post successfully. It was only when another user responded to my message that I knew I had succeeded, and this gave me a great sense of relief." (Student 3 – from Personal essay).

Electronic discussion groups, whether asynchronous or synchronous, allow students and teachers to communicate on a level that erases the tradition of 'sage on a stage' and encourages students to express their own ideas and opinions. Walther equates this with egalitarianism and Baron finds that the format of CMC makes it difficult for people to dominate and impose their views on the group (Walther, 1992; Baron, 1984).

Again, comments from the Technological Innovations students support this:

> "The sense of equality has been one of the most appealing and encouraging features of using the bulletin board. I have been able to quickly establish myself as a regular contributor without feeling intimidated by other students." (Student 11 – from Personal essay).

Hiltz and Turoff provide a detailed review of dated, but nevertheless relevant, work carried out in this area (Hiltz and Turoff, 1993). In several cases they have replicated the experimental research. They suggest, for example, that face-to-face group work can be dominated by a small subset of individuals and frequently a single leader emerges. Reporting experimental work based on Interaction Process Analysis, they suggest that domination and leadership are predicated on an individual's ability to respond rapidly and grab turns in a discussion - their Latency of Verbal Response (LVR) - rather than on intelligence (as measured by IQ) or personality. By its nature, CMC negates this problem and as a result multiple group leaders often emerge based on functional strengths.

"...however, there were times which I found it difficult
[sic] with the online discussion. Perhaps due to the time
available to think over, at times there would be someone
who would say a lot in one go...This sometimes made
me very tempted to skip or scan through it very
quickly...." (Student 12 – from Personal essay).

Research also shows that this lack of domination makes it difficult
for a group consensus to be formed or for a task to be completed (Hiltz and
Turoff, 1993; Sproull and Kiesler, 1991). Groups are inclined to produce a
greater range of opinions and there is less of a tendency to agree than in
face-to-face groups. It seems likely that these findings are linked to the
idea that CMC gives participants greater control over their public image. In
discussing the use of anonymity and pseudonymity in CMC, Feenberg
draws on Goffman's notion of a doubly-defined self - as public image or
identity *and* as a sacred object (Feenberg, 1989). CMC appears to promote
control over image whilst reducing the risk of embarrassment. Participants
thus feel more able to speak their minds and less constrained to conform to
an expected norm.

"....paradoxically, although my contributions would be
made in text and preserved throughout the module for all
to see, studying in cyberspace would allow me to hide
my lack of academic experience...Cyberspace would
buy me time to prepare decent responses and
contributions." (Student 7 – from Personal essay).

Critics of CMC point to the narrowing of communication
channels and the absence of many of the cues normally associated with
face-to-face communication. Communicating using text from remote
locations means participants in a discussion are without audio and visual
cues.

"When attending classes in the past, personalities of
individuals have become clear (including those of the
teaching staff) and relationships have developed. This
also resulted in non-verbal feedback during the
year...This feedback was obviously not going to be there
when using the bulletin board alone." (Student 8 – from
Personal essay).

However, although the richness of the interaction is missing,
participants do seem able to make up for their lost senses, for example

through the use of emoticons (such as smileys). Kaye acknowledges a lack of para-linguistic cues in CMC group activities but goes on to describe CMC as richer than many other forms of textual communication and as a medium that combines the advantages of verbal communication with the permanency and re-use of writing (Kaye, 1992). Hiltz and Turoff offer evidence that the narrowing of communication channels may actually promote contribution and rationality in certain forms of task (Hiltz and Turoff, 1993). They also suggest that the absence of cues can help to mask an individual from a group. Anonymity, or the use of a pseudonym, takes this to the extreme. Hiltz and Turoff report research that suggests that this can lead to the promotion of effective group activity through the subordination of an individual's self to the task of the group (Hiltz and Turoff, 1993). This is demonstrated in the following:

> "However, the class homepage proved itself useful to bridge this [feedback] gap as individual class members (and the lecturer) were able to be contacted by e-mail to ask any questions outside of the bulletin board." (Student 8 - from Personal essay).

In the Technological Innovations module there were two synchronous chat sessions during the semester in addition to the postings on the BBS. The first chat session was held approximately one month into the semester. By this time students had begun to know each other from introductions on the BBS and from the daily exchange of opinions and discussion in the asynchronous environment. The first chat session was held during the week in which self-identity in an online environment was one of the topics. It was also the week of Halloween. It was decided to have an online 'costume party'. Each student would come into the synchronous web based chat room wearing a virtual costume (a screen handle instead of their real name). There was no set topic for discussion; instead they were supposed to chat with each other and try to guess identities. Students were also told not to assume a different persona but rather to treat the experience as an opportunity to gain familiarity with a synchronous chat environment. Prior to this session there were only three or four students who had chat room experience.

> "...We did not have a specific topic for the discussion which created anarchy, however, I was able to familiarise myself with the technology and identify ways of maximising the effectiveness of the system ready for my second chat room session...." (Student 11 -from Personal essay).

Moore's theory of transactional distance education states that the more dialogue in a course the less structure there will be and vice versa (Moore, 1973; Moore, 1993). An online class discussion will have much dialogue but little structure unless the instructor defines the topic and rules for discussion prior to the online conference. For a group discussion to be productive in concrete terms there must be a tight structure on the nature of the dialogue and of the tasks that are to be completed during the allotted time frame.

The second synchronous 'chat' session saw the group divided into two smaller groups that met on different nights. The session was also structured around an initial set of questions to begin the discussion. Students were able to stay on task and follow a discussion even when some students experienced difficulty with the chat room software.

> "...I came to feel that chat rooms, set up correctly with clear objectives, clear rules of engagement, and an acknowledged chair to keep dissidents (in terms of the agreed subject matter) on track, can be an exceptionally focussed, time-efficient and productive method communication." (Student 13 – from Personal essay).

Kearsley and Lynch find that the single most important instrument of structure in any course, whether it is taught at a distance or traditionally, is the course syllabus (Kearsley and Lynch, 1997). A well designed syllabus outlines the goals and objectives of the course, prerequisites, the grading and evaluation schemes, materials to be used, topics to be covered and a schedule.

> "I thought the module was extremely well put together. The material was well presented and structured and I always knew what was expected. This was extremely important as the module was online. It would have been quite easy to have felt lost – and at times I did – but the structure of the home page was like an anchor that you could secure yourself to." (Student 3 – from Questionnaire).

Kearsley and Lynch go on to state that whereas the amount of structure in a distance education course is determined by the instructor, ambiguity in the syllabus usually results in student anxiety. The nature of the presentation of material can reduce this anxiety as students who are in computer conferencing with the instructor on a regular basis can ask for clarification as the course progresses.

"The tutor's interventions on the bulletin board were also
important and well timed – I needed to know that she
was taking an active interest. I won't pretend that I didn't
find it difficult – I most certainly did – but I think that
taught me a lot …" (Student 3 – from Questionnaire).

The Technological Innovations class was tightly structured so that
students would know what they were supposed to do each week. Each
weekly class session had its own web page that had links to a series of
newspaper and magazine articles about the week's topic. The guest for the
week was introduced and there was an initial question to start the
discussion. As well as the initial discussion question, students were set an
exercise (such as following Ebay auctions the week e-commerce was
discussed). They were encouraged to integrate the exercises into the
discussions about the readings.

2.   Method

Many colleges and universities around the world have been using
the World Wide Web to either support traditional face-to-face teaching or
have been branching out into the actual delivery of courses online. This
study focuses on a group of MA students at a UK university in the
Midlands.

The students in this study were taking their first class in either an
MA in Interactive Multimedia (IM) or E-Business (E-Biz), none had
previously taken a class at a distance. The class was equally divided
between full time, part time, and IM and E-Biz students. Twenty-one
percent were at the traditional age for entering postgraduate education
directly from an undergraduate degree. The semester began with nineteen
students. The students dropped out during the course of the semester, all of
whom were part-time students. This is not uncommon with part time
students since they sometimes find that the combination of work load and
study is more than they expected.

Students participated in an online seminar that used both
synchronous and asynchronous methods for communicating. They were
also required to work in pairs on a project. At the end of the semester the
students wrote an essay documenting their expectations and experiences of
working and communicating in cyberspace. They also completed a self-
assessment of learning instrument that is not distant learning specific. Here
is an example of a comment from the self assessment returns and illustrates
a typical student attitude:

"… I was feeling apprehensive, as I had no experience of
how to conduct myself in such an environment. Thoughts

going round my head included concerns of being ignored, not being taken seriously or generally not fitting in with the crowd." (Student 5 – from Personal essay)

The objectives of the class were to acquaint the student with the social and economic impacts of new communication technologies. This subject matter lends itself quite well to an online discussion. Not only were students studying many of the issues surrounding adoption and design of multimedia, they were actually experiencing them. To make sure that there was adequate online discussion the students were informed that participation was worth 30% of their final grade. It was stressed that the participation grade was a quantitative one and not a qualitative one. The more the student posted to the BBS, the higher his/her participation grade. The average number of postings per student was 6.7 each week.

> "Getting behind is not an option and this can lead to
> stress, anxiety and ultimately not getting work done ..."
> (Student 10 – from personal essay)

The semester was divided into ten weeks for discussion. Each week had a different topic and a different guest. Guests were experts in the subject matter for the week and were invited to participate in the discussion.

Approximately one semester after completing the online class, students were emailed a self-assessment questionnaire about their participation in the online class. The time delay was to allow students a chance to experience more traditional postgraduate classes as this online class was their first postgraduate experience. Sixteen students were emailed the questionnaire with thirteen of them returning it. The questionnaire was set up on a standard five point Likert scale with 1 being a low score and 5 being a high score.

One question (Question 5: "I learned how to solve problems") was rated low by nearly all of the students, because they felt that they already had experience in this and that the module didn't help or hurt them in this area.

> "... I have already had quite extensive experience of
> problem solving in both my teaching and industry
> employment and feel this module was geared more
> toward exploration and new ideas than problem solving."
> (Student 6 – from questionnaire).

This question needs to be followed up because one of the assignments the students complete is a problem-solving one. They choose another student with whom to work and are required to complete an structured informational website surrounding one of the issues discussed during the semester. The problem-solving nature of the assignment is that they are only to work in cyberspace. No face-to-face meetings and no telephone calls are permitted in completing the assignment. Many of the students have difficulty in completing this assignment:

> "... I learned valuable lessons about myself here. I am not a 'joint' person. Both parties were heavily time-committed elsewhere, and asynchronous communication was a tremendous aid to the time availability problem. However, further difficulties arose with ageing home-based hardware and restrictive protection in the work environment. What should have been a simple exercise became a nightmare of e-complexities...." (Student 9 - from personal essay).

3.   **Summary of questionnaire data:**

Students were generally equally divided by gender, course of study and part-time or full-time status.

Table 1. Respondents by gender and study mode

	Part-time	Full-time	
Male	3	4	7
Female	5	1	6
	8	5	13

Table 2. Respondents by gender and course

	E-Business	IM	
Male	3	4	7
Female	4	2	6
	7	6	13

Table 3. Respondents by study mode and course

	E-Business	IM	
Part-time	7	1	8
Full-time	0	5	5
	8	5	13

The questionnaire comprised ten questions. The first eight asked the student to rate their response on a standard Likert scale with one being low and five being high. Questions 9 and 10 were open ended questions asking students to pick a response they rated low and high and to give an explanation. As such they could not be analysed in a similar manner to the other eight.

Table 4. Mean question scores – all respondents

Q1 My intellectual curiosity was stimulated by this module.	4.15
Q2 I learned to think more clearly about this subject area.	4.08
Q3* This module helped me express myself more effectively.	3.77
Q4* I learned to gather information relevant to a problem.	3.85
Q5 I learned how to solve problems.	2.77
Q6* I connected what I learned in this module with my experience in other modules or outside of university.	4.08
Q7 I participated by listening, talking, and being prepared for class.	3.85
Q8* Overall, my learning in this module was aided by the instructor's activities, materials, assignments, and presentations.	4.38

* = questions relating to student satisfaction

Standard t-tests for difference of means were used to explore the possibility of differences between intra-group responses as defined by gender, study mode and course (Moore et al, 1972). The null hypothesis (H_0) was tested in all cases. Thus, H_0 assumes that any difference that exists between mean response scores, for example between those of male and female students, is due only to sampling variation and not to any real difference in the populations from which the samples are drawn.

Where the calculated t-value exceeds the critical value from tables, H_0 can be rejected and a significant difference in populations can be said to exist (Hoel, 1976). Where the t-test does not reject H_0 then, with a given level of probability, it may be assumed that no real differences between sample responses exist and that the samples are drawn from one and the same population.

The t-tests show no evidence of differences in responses between male and female students (H_0 is not rejected). However, when considering the responses from E-business and Interactive Multimedia students H_0 is rejected and differences are significant at the 10% level. In other words, there is a 90% probability that differences in the mean response scores between students of the two courses are due to something other than sampling error. H_0 is rejected when responses are considered by study mode and differences are seen to be significant at the 5% level (a 95% probability that differences are not due to sampling error).

Table 5. t-tests for difference of means based on ALL responses

Degrees of freedom (DF) = $n_1 + n_2 - 2 = 11$			
Critical values: 2.201 @ 5% level & 1.796 @10% level			
GENDER	Male v female	t = 0.741	NS at 5% level
STUDY MODE	part-time v full-time	t = 2.405	Significant at 5% level
COURSE	E-biz v Int Media	t = 1.978	Significant at 10% level

Table 6. t-tests for difference of means based on responses to satisfaction questions *

Degrees of freedom (DF) = $n_1 + n_2 - 2 = 11$			
Critical values: 2.201 @ 5% level & 1.796 @10% level			
GENDER	Male v female	t = 1.011	NS at 5% level
STUDY MODE	part-time v full-time	t = 2.197	Significant at 10% level
COURSE	E-biz v Int Media	t = 1.813	Significant at 10% level

That the E-business course is made up entirely of part-time students (7 of 7) when considered with the *t*-test results suggests the critical differentiator of attitudes to virtual learning environments is the study mode - part-time or full-time. Clearly, it may not be the study mode but the typical characteristics of those who choose to study in each mode that is most important. Although a more focused study is needed to investigate this fully, a correlation coefficient (Pearson product-moment) of the association between total response scores and work experience measured in years was calculated and is presented in Table 7 (Salkind, 2003).

Table 7. Pearson product-moment coefficient

All questions – total response score and work experience
Pearson product-moment coefficient = 0.79581952.
This represents a significant relationship at the 5% level (0.553).

4. Summary

Results show that students who were re-entering higher education after a number of years adapted to the 'any time, any place' mode of asynchronous teaching with a higher level of satisfaction than traditional students. Traditional students also wanted more synchronous online meetings and felt more isolated during the learning experience.

> "…it might have been useful if there were one or two face to face meetings of the class so that we had a more personal contact and approach with others." (Student 2 – from Personal essay).

The non-traditional students were intimidated by the educational experiences of the traditional students and the traditional students were intimidated by the work experience of the non-traditional students.

> "Not coming from an academic background I was feeling very apprehensive." (Student 7 – from Personal essay).
> "It seemed to me that the E-Business members were more confident and better informed and all together more active on the bulletin board than the interactive media members. This I found a little intimidating." (Student 6 – from Personal essay).

A computer-mediated environment allows members of different groups the opportunity to have their voice heard. Feelings of face-to-face intimidation can be avoided in an online classroom provided the instructor has created an atmosphere where students feel that they are in control of the learning space and learning experience.

Is, then, CMC any better at promoting learning than traditional modes of communication? It certainly helps deliver educational programmes to people who would otherwise not be in a position to take part. It also helps put large numbers of students in touch with their peers and teachers and promotes student-student and student-teacher dialogue in an environment of mass higher education. So, as an alternative to other, less practical modes of communication the answer must be that, yes, CMC is indeed better at promoting learning.

References

Acker, S. (1994), 'Space, collaboration, and the credible city: Academic work in the virtual community', *Journal of computer mediated communication.* 1.

http://cwis.usc.edu/dept/annenberg/vol1/issue1/acker/acktext.htm
(Accessed 20 December 2000)

Baron, N.S. (1984), 'Computer mediated communication as a force in language change', *Visible language.* 18: 118-141.

Feenberg, A. (1989), 'The written world: on the theory and practice of computer conferencing', in: Mason, R.D. and Kaye, A.R. (eds.) *Mindweave: Communication, computers and distance education.* Oxford: Pergamon. 22-39.

Hiltz, S.R. and Turoff, M. (1993), *The network nation: Human communication via computer.* Cambridge, MA: MIT Press.

Kaye, A.R. (1989), 'Computer-mediated communication and distance education', in: Mason, R.D. and Kaye, A.R. (eds.) *Mindweave: Communication, computers and distance education.* Oxford: Pergamon.

Kaye, A.R. (1992), 'Learning together apart', in: Kaye, A.R. (ed.) *Collaborative learning through computer conferencing: the Najaden papers.* Berlin: Springer-Verlag. 1-23.

Kearsley, G. and Lynch W. (1997), 'Structural issues in distance education', *Journal of education for business.* 4: 191.

Moore, P G, Erly A C Shirley, and D E Edwards. *Standard Statistical Calculations.* London: Pitman, 1972.

Moore, M.G. (1973), 'Towards a theory of independent learning in higher education', *Journal of higher education.* 44: 661-679.

Moore, M. G. (1993), 'Theory of transactional distance', in: D. Keegan (ed.) *Theoretical principles of distance education.* New York: Routledge.

Salkind, N.J. (2003), *Exploring Research.* Upper Saddle River, NJ: Prentice Hall.

Sproull, L. and Kiesler, S. (1991), *Connections: New ways of working in the networked organisation.* Cambridge, MA: MIT Press.

Walther, J.B. (1992), 'Interpersonal effects in computer-mediated interaction', *Communication research.* 19: 52-90.

Going From Distance to Digital: Athabasca University's E-Learning Plan

Lynda R. Ross and Alan Davis

Abstract

Athabasca University (AU), Canada's Open University, has experienced significant growth in student enrollments, course offerings and staff since its inception in 1970. In 2001/02 AU enrolled approximately 24,000 students in nearly 550 courses from 29 undergraduate and five graduate programmes. Staff include 104 full-time and 117 part-time academics, 249 academic tutors and nearly 500 other workers (professionals, managers/executive officers, support, temporary and casual staff). AU's mission has always focussed on the removal of barriers for those unable to access university education and on excellence in teaching and research. In the fall of 2001, AU began development of a new Strategic University Plan (SUP) to cover the period from 2002 to 2006. Integral to the SUP was a commitment to the use of technology to improve access and to remove barriers to learning and a significant expansion of online infrastructures to support e-learning throughout North America. The SUP also anticipates: an expansion in broadband infrastructure; an increased presence and u``sability of e-books and related technology; an expanded involvement of the commercial publishing industry in interactive, multimedia learning resources. In concert with the SUP, the E-Learning Plan (ELP) was created to provide direction for the development of e-learning at AU. The ELP proposes a shift from an undergraduate course development system based primarily on individualised study relying on print materials, telephone/e-mail tutoring and optional online derivatives (course outlines, frequently asked questions, quizzes and so on) to a system that regards the online learning environment as primary. Course materials, learning activities, and tutoring models will consequently be designed with this orientation in mind. Although every AU course is currently offered with some online components, the goal for the year 2005 is for all undergraduate courses to include proven online learning and assessment activities. The strategies AU will use, and the challenges it will face to achieve this goal, are the subjects of this chapter.

1. Introduction

Like other post-secondary institutions in Canada and worldwide, AU has not been immune to the pull of technology. However, unlike many other universities and colleges, as Canada's Open University, AU brings a great deal of history and experience as a provider of high quality distance education to the challenge of online teaching and learning. In moving towards a fully online design and delivery platform for distance education, AU continues to explore the evolving role of higher education in society as well as the needs for new relationships between education and business (Berg, 1998). There is no doubt that the expanded use of computer and network technologies to deliver instruction and provide students with access to information resources will change higher education in significant ways including its organisational relationships, financial operations, student participation patterns and faculty roles (Wallhaus, 2000). The vision and goals for education, however, remain the same, regardless of the medium or delivery mode, and in planning for and conceptualising the shift to online delivery, AU's understandings about the meaning of education will not change. University education is fundamentally concerned with broadening students' intellectual horizons both by providing opportunities for the pursuit of truth, comprehension and generation of new and complex ideas, discovery of meaning, and by ensuring students exercise emotional maturity and use good judgement. Ultimately, education is about providing the forum for the development of wisdom (Burniske and Monke, 2001). Acknowledging the inevitability of the trend to online learning, the practical issues for traditional or distance learning institutions of moving to online teaching and learning environments should be viewed only as complications inherent in the transition process (Johnson and DeSpain, 2001). Thus the greatest challenges to developing e-learning curricula are neither administrative nor technological - although these areas present demands of their own - but instead concern notions governing the fundamental and broader purpose of post-secondary education.

In 2001 the Advisory Committee on Online Learning (ACOL) noted the

> "...importance of lifelong learning to success in a knowledge-based society and the potential of new learning tools both to enrich traditional teaching and to extend lifelong learning opportunities to Canadians in all walks of life." (ACOL, 2001, iv)

Opinion about the effects on post-secondary institutions of choosing or not choosing to adapt to the new e-learning technologies varies. Some have claimed that failure to adapt to the e-learning challenge will result in "... declining enrolments, smaller grants from government and thus less capacity for institutions to fulfil their role as an intellectual resource and educator for provinces, territories and communities" (ACOL, 2001, 4). Demands for post-secondary institutions to adopt online teaching and learning strategies come from a variety of public and private sectors and are complicated to some extent by a lack of real knowledge about the processes and consequences of e-teaching and e-learning. There is no doubt that the educational community is being bombarded by hyperbole surrounding the information super-highway (Burniske and Monke, 2001). Post-secondary institutions are constantly subjected to a barrage of information from hundreds of commercial Web-based companies offering educators various tools for designing and managing courses online (Mann, 2000a). Tools are being marketed on the basis of a multitude of technical specifications, instructional design values, media capabilities, ease of use and potential for collaboration and connectivity (WICHE, 2002). A plethora of how-to manuals, books and articles have appeared in the past few years, offering so-called expert advice on designing, developing and delivering online courses, on training programmes, on marketing, and on managing e-learning options. In most instances, these how-to manuals have preceded new instructional theories that could offer guidance as to how distance learning technologies can and should be used with greatest effectiveness. Colleges and universities, as one author suggests, appear to be "...rushing at an alarming rate to answer the call of the growing number of online learners" (Gibbons and Wentworth, 2001, 1). There is no doubt that "e-learning is a rapidly expanding category of e-business" (Oblinger and Katz, 2000, 4) and AU would be foolish if it were not concerned about the commodification and the corruption that the new commercial ethos could bring to public higher education (Noble, 1997; Noble, 1998a; Noble, 1998b; Noble, 1999).

As a commercial venture, the prospects for e-learning providers appear to be unlimited and many institutions seem to be motivated by the promise of financial rewards (Johnson and DeSpain, 2000; Oblinger and Katz, 2000). The concept of the virtual university has already been implemented in 33 of the United States of America (Johnson and DeSpain, 2000). In Canada, a survey conducted by Campus Computing International between March 1999 and May 2000

> "...revealed that 57% of Canada's 134 colleges and universities offer online courses. The institutions offer almost 3000 courses altogether ranging from one to 340 courses for each institution." (ACOL, 2001, 30)

The pull of technology is evident. However, AU is not so much committed to responding to these pulls - although in today's climate they are impossible to ignore - but instead to pushing judiciously the effective use of technology, by continuing to use it in innovative ways, by exploring new possibilities, by researching its own as well as the experiences of others and by using and disseminating the results of these efforts. AU's commitment is to influence rather than simply to react to the use of technology. As a first concrete step in controlling its e-learning destiny and in the implementation of an integrated e-learning environment, AU recently developed an E-Learning Plan (ELP). The remainder of this chapter will highlight the process and goals of, the plan for and the challenges facing the ELP. Before doing so, the next few sections will provide the context for the ELP with a cursory description of AU, its structure and governance, its mission, its approach to course development and its current Strategic University Plan.

2.   Athabasca University
A.   Past and Present

Located in a small office building in the city of Edmonton in northern Alberta, Athabasca University began its first pilot project in distance education in November of 1972. There were two staff members with plans to develop three introductory level courses, one in World Ecology, a second introducing the Study of Human Communities, and a third exploring the Ancient Roots of the Modern World. By the fall of 1973 the World Ecology course was opened to 160 students and by the end of the pilot project in 1975 there were 534 course registrations in these three courses. At that time, AU was operating with five academic staff and 11 instructional designers, editors, and visual designers as well as 15 support staff (Abrioux, 2001a).

From these humble beginnings AU has experienced significant growth in terms of student population, curriculum, and staffing. Full-time equivalent registrations have increased to 4,342, representing 43,420 individual course enrollments. The actual student population in 2001/02 was approximately 24,000 (with graduate registrations representing just over 13% of the total). In the same year 298 undergraduate and 278 graduate degrees were awarded. The curriculum has expanded to 546 courses in 29 undergraduate degree and certificate programmes and five graduate programmes. Liberal Arts and Sciences still dominate the curriculum, although the proportion of Applied and Professional courses has increased marginally over the last five year period. As of March 2002 there was a total of 919 staff members including 104 full-time academics and 117 part-time academics. There were also 115 professional staff, 15 management/executive officers, 251 support and temporary staff, 68 casual staff and 249 course tutors (AU, 2002).

B.   Structure and Governance

With the revision of the Alberta Universities Act in 1978, AU was granted permanent self-governing status. Decision-making rests with the Athabasca University Governing Council (AUGC) in a unicameral governance system. Overall, academic policy is delegated to AU's

Academic Council. AU is a publicly funded university and reports to the Government of Alberta through the Minister of Alberta Learning. There are fourteen undergraduate and graduate academic centres and eighteen administrative and service units within AU and there are a variety of internal academic subcommittees of Academic Council (such as the Undergraduate Studies Board and the Graduate Studies Board) with direct policy decisions requiring the final approval by AUGC.

C.   The University's Mission

AU's mission statement has changed little from its adoption in 1985 and it dedicates the university "...to the removal of barriers that restrict access to and success in university-level studies and to increasing equality of educational opportunity for adult learners worldwide" (AU, 2002, 5). Like other universities in Canada, AU "...is committed to excellence in teaching, research, and scholarship, and to being of service to the general public" (AU, 2002, 5).

D.   Approach to Course Development and Delivery

As AU is a distance education provider, course offerings are primarily delivered in print-based format, supplemented by telephone and e-mail access to course tutors, library and student services. Some courses also have audio and video as well as online materials. Although AU offers some courses in grouped study mode, either in classrooms or via the Web, 90% of AU students take courses in the individualised study mode. Grouped study requires students to register at set times during the year (fall, winter, spring and summer semesters) and cover materials in a paced manner, whereas students pursuing individualised study may register at any time during the year and they may self-pace their studies within the limits of the course contract (6 months for a 3-credit course or 12 months for a 6-credit course).

AU has for a number of years followed a formal Seven-Phase Plan for course development. As part of a strategy to maintain AU's leadership in the design, development and deployment of print as well digital technologies for education and research, AU's Educational Media Development (EMD) department was established in 1995. EMD is mandated to provide the university community with the administrative, creative and technical infrastructure to design, develop and deliver high-quality courseware to students. Twenty-five staff members provide instructional, multimedia, visual and graphic design, copyright clearance, editing and typesetting services as well as a variety of instructional technology services to assist in the course development process. Given the rapid evolution of relevant technologies, departmental staff are also engaged in pilot projects, experimentation and training to ensure that their knowledge remains current in their fields.

Although the Seven-Phase Plan was originally developed with print-based materials in mind, this process will continue to guide online course development at AU. The first of the seven phases assesses needs at the programme level and is concerned with long-range educational planning taking direction from the Strategic University Plan to determine the criteria by which new or existing programmes are developed, revised or cancelled. Phase 2 identifies the courses required to meet specific demands of the first phase. Planning is based on the approval of proposals developed according to guidelines set by Academic Council and Alberta Learning.

The remaining five phases are focussed on the specifics of courses approved for development. Phase 3 involves course plans which includes details of all relevant components and structure of proposed new courses (such as course objectives, unit summaries, learning objectives, study questions, readings, texts, assignments, exams and quizzes) as well as a completed sample unit. In addition, delivery modes, costs, and resources required to develop the course are itemised in the report. All Phase 3s are circulated for discussion and peer review among academic and non-academic centres. On recommendation of the Centre's Chair, Phase 3s are approved - or not - by the Vice President Academic (VPA). If approved, the course proceeds to Phase 4 in which course materials are prepared, in accordance with the course specifications described in the Phase 3, by academic experts in consultation with editors, visual designers, copyright officers and, when appropriate, with multimedia instructional designers. Phase 5 involves the actual delivery of the course undertaken according to the detailed specifications described in Phase 3.

Phase 6 focusses on evaluating the teaching effectiveness of the course. This is accomplished through student and tutor feedback, assessments of course registration data and, when warranted, through formal course and programme evaluations. Evaluation results are reported to the Centre Chair and the VPA. Course revisions, the responsibility of the course coordinator, occur during Phase 7. Courses are assessed annually with regard to the relevance and accuracy of the texts and other purchased materials (such as audio and video cassettes and CD-ROMs), tests and assignments, rigour of course content and transferability to other universities. Revisions are conducted based on these criteria.

3.   AU's Current Strategic University Plan
In order to guide strategic university planning, a steering committee was struck in the fall of 2001. Following a series of discussions, university-wide forums, drafts and revisions, a final version of the SUP was approved by AUGC in June 2002. Key strategic issues addressed by

the SUP included AU's social mission, growth, learning models, learner support services, research, technology and telecommunications, organisational development and fiscal policy and included a focus on performance indicators (Abrioux, 2001b). Critical to the university's E-Learning Plan (ELP) was the mandate established by the SUP stating that the period covering 2002 to 2006

> "...will be characterized by use of technology to improve access and to remove barriers to learning; significant expansion of online infrastructures in support of e-learning throughout North America; expanded broadband infrastructure; increased presence and usability of e-books and related technology; and expanded involvement of the commercial publishing industry in interactive, multimedia learning resources." (AU, 2002, 4)

The new SUP further focussed AU's e-learning strategies through the following directives:

> "All undergraduate courses will include proven, online-learning and online-assessment activities and resources by developing and implementing an E-Learning Plan and by using digital systems to increase the flexibility and access to learning resources, where proven successful." (AU, 2002, 5)

While the directives from the SUP were clear, emphasis on the word 'proven' has led to a great deal of debate within the institution. This debate includes issues surrounding technological choices, workload, and training, but most importantly focuses on the interactions between new pedagogies and the use of technologies to enhance teaching and learning.

4.   AU's E-Learning Plan

The ELP, with its focus primarily on undergraduate course development and delivery, was created as the basis for the implementation and evaluation of AU's online course development goals. The plan is also designed to act as a bridge between the broad goals of the SUP and the operational plans of various service and academic units within the university. In September of 2001, in tandem with strategic university planning activity, an E-Learning steering committee was struck under the direction of the VPA. The committee, composed of 12 members from various academic and service centres, was directed to establish a clear plan to guide the university in its online development for the next five year period.

The ELP defines a multi-dimensional framework in an effort to strike a balance between all of the critical elements necessary for creating successful teaching and learning environments online while acknowledging the constraints and challenges to be faced in operationalising such a large scale project. While the plan is an ambitious one, without systematic attention to key strategic areas such as market research, planning, coordination, pedagogy and standards, work practice, technology and technological skills, policy, resources, and student access issues, such a large-scale online project would be doomed to failure from the outset (Ellis and Phelps, 2000; Gerson, 2000). Without integrated frameworks reflecting priorities, strategies, and values of the institution, there can be no success of e-learning projects in post-secondary education institutions (Bates, 2000; Katz, 2000; McAlister et al, 2001; Yeung, 2002). Furthermore, the single most important issue in promoting online education on mission driven campuses seems to be how well online projects support the universities' mission statements (Rahman, 2001). The removal of barriers and the the increasing of student access to post-secondary education are the primary reasons for AU's pursuit of excellence in developing online teaching and learning strategies.

Post-secondary institutions generally seem to follow two different approaches to managing online course development. One approach has faculty members working alone or in collaboration with other colleagues within individual departments to develop online learning and delivery systems. The other approach takes place in institutions where there is collaboration within and between academic departments as well as with selected university service units in order to implement the conversion process (Care and Scanlan, 2001). To date, online conversion at AU has seen both approaches. Largely however, with the exception of the graduate programmes, online conversion at AU has occurred on a somewhat ad hoc basis. AU has been a very successful provider of distance education, primarily in a print-based mode. This experience allows AU to draw upon existing systems in preparation for a full-scale conversion to online course development and delivery while recognising that the implementation of e-learning strategies will require redesign of materials and review and revision of current policies and procedures (particularly as they affect course design and delivery) as well as a possible re-evaluation of policies and processes related to faculty development, evaluation and workload (Kidwell et al, 2000). Although the ELP provides explicit time-lines for the conversion process, online conversions will not proceed without careful consideration, constant evaluation and necessary readjustments to the plan.

The ELP recognises that a plan is, after all, just a plan and leaves room for reassessment and reevaluation when and where necessary.

Various authors have suggested the need for theoretically informed online learning systems and Web-course management (Mann, 2000b). Although there is little substantive theory in the literature and few well-planned empirical studies dealing with online pedagogy, Mann provides a three phase approach that institutions might follow in order to facilitate Web-course development and management (Mann, 2000b). The first phase suggests the use of online lesson and course enhancements based on instructors' intuitive understandings. Such enhancements are categorised by Mann as collaborative environments, opportunities for instructors to express themselves online and the inclusion of online student assessments. Mann describes the second phase of development as online resource-based learning. This phase is defined by any online teaching resources or knowledge information provided by the instructor, available for retrieval by the student, to enhance the learning objectives of the course. As the third and final phase of Web course management, Mann suggests a learning environment defined as "...a virtual space where learners work together and support one another as they use a variety of tools and information resources in pursuit of learning goals and problem-solving activities" (Mann, 2000b, 17). Such terms as exploration, experimentation, construction and knowledge transformation, all of which support the goals and visions of higher education, characterise this environment. This final and full phase of online course development and delivery also complies with constructivist notions of learner-centred teaching pedagogies which have been lauded as the single greatest advantage of Web-based instruction.

A.   Survey of Academic Centres

After the establishment of the ELP steering committee, and as a second concrete step in the process, a survey of AU's nine Academic Centres was undertaken in October of 2001. The survey was designed to assess the extent to which courses and programmes within various centres considered themselves to be online. The survey also acted as a systematic 'stock-taking' method, not only of the extent of online course development at AU, but also of the range of tools and platforms that were currently in use. AU's graduate programmes have been teaching groups online for the past five years and a number of undergraduate academic centres at AU can be considered as early-adopters of e-technology. Centres were asked to identify how many of their individualised study courses had online components ranging from simple informational components (Web course page linked to centre Web page, course syllabus, staff information), through slightly more detailed but still in the category of informational components (links to readings, links to other resources) to somewhat more interactive (links to quizzes and self-tests) and finally to fully interactive course-specific components (interactive Java applets, video streaming, learning objects).

The results of the survey indicated a significant range in the number of courses containing online components across the nine academic centres. Most courses that were identified as containing simple informational as well as detailed informational online components also reported a variety of interactive components online. Centres reported a range of between four percent (Global and Social Analysis) and 100% (Psychology, Centre for Computing and Information Systems) of their courses with these levels of online components. Fewer courses across the various centres reported more sophisticated and interactive course specific components that would be typical of Mann's specified second and third phases of online course management. The majority of centres reported that none of their courses met this criterion although one centre - Computing and Information Systems - reported 40% of their courses meeting this criterion. Many of the academic centres reported using Web resources that were not tied to specific courses or content.

Academic centres also reported using a broad range of tools to create online learning environments, course enhancements, Web resources not specifically tied to courses (such as Fireworks, Dreamweaver, Macromedia, Flash, Photoshop, XML Spy, Linux, HTML, Adobe Illustrator) as well as a variety of different platforms used to deliver and manage courses (LotusNotes, WebCT, Domino, Bazaar, WWWBoard). Less than one third of the centres reported providing any online orientation to either students or course tutors. Only two of the nine centres were keeping formal records measuring student online activity related to course components and use of Web resources not specifically tied to courses. In terms of measuring the effectiveness of online course components and Web resources to student learning, about one half of the centres reported employing formal course evaluations while the remainder relied on informal feedback such as complaints, grades and pass rates. Students' experiences with the online components were also, for most centres, assessed by reliance on informal rather than formal feedback.

The goal of the ELP was to present a series of recommendations and strategies for online course development to the university's governing bodies and to the university community at large by the end of March 2002. The ELP committee began with informed notions about the direction AU would take regarding online course development and delivery as well as knowledge of the challenges to be faced in implementing such a large scale project. With AU's experience of online development and delivery, the ELP acknowledged the need to bring coherence to its overall approach to online course development and delivery and to prepare for continuing evolutions of online systems. Part of the ELP strategy involves a systematic evaluation of the effectiveness of what has already taken place in grouped and individualised online study at AU. In addition, the ELP identified a need to limit the number of production platforms employed while leaving opportunity for innovation for research and pilot project experimentation. In relation to this, the ELP also identified a need to continue to assess trends and products most likely to bring added effectiveness and efficiencies to online development and delivery as well as a need to investigate optimal integration of course production and delivery systems.

An initial ELP report was drafted and submitted to various AU governing bodies at the end of December 2001. This report was based on discussions within the steering committee and findings from the survey of the academic centres. Following this submission the ELP team continued to meet on a regular basis. During the spring of 2002, several university-wide forums were held to discuss the draft report which included strategies for implementing the ELP. Throughout the process, faculty and non-faculty members were encouraged to comment directly to the VPA. Relevant comments and concerns were integrated into the final plan.

B.   E-Learning Goals for Course Development and Delivery
        The final ELP document set the broad goal of having all undergraduate courses designed, developed and delivered online to individual learners by 2006. Recognising that off-line options will continue to be needed for some students (those unable to connect to the University for example) the plan takes into account the need to derive print-based delivery materials and suggests these materials will be produced in a just-in-time basis from primary online course components. Whereas some undergraduate centres, such as the School of Business, have been experimenting with grouped e-learning classes, in the future, grouped online courses or grouped activities within individualised courses will only be used to serve clearly identified student populations or to meet specific and essential learning outcomes. Generally accepted principles for good practice in teaching and learning will drive the design and development of all courses. As has always been evident in AU's print-based course development and delivery strategies, these practices include: encouraging contact between students and faculty; the use of active learning and assessment techniques; provision of prompt feedback; the setting of clear learning objectives and expectations; providing access to support services; and respect for diverse talents and ways of learning that students bring with them to their studies (Bower, 2001; Essex and Cagiltay, 2001; Gordon, 2000; MacDonald, 2001). In addition, development of reciprocity and

cooperation among students has been cited, in relation to online learning, as a good teaching and learning practice (Edelstein and Edwards, 2002).

'E-learning' is a broad term. In the context of the ELP it is being used as an umbrella to cover the online and digital systems and resources AU uses to design, develop and deliver course offerings as well as student services. Any discussion of course quality must include not only components relevant to specific courses but must also take into account issues related to access to resources such as library, labs and student services as well as life experiences designed for student socialisation and affective development via student-to-student interaction (Edelstein and Edwards, 2002; Palloff and Pratt, 1999). The online environment presents the ultimate challenge of how computer technology is going to be used to help "...students develop those inner qualities such as insight, creativity and good judgement, which education at its best has always sought to inspire" (Burniske and Monke, 2001, 19).

In addition to teaching and learning challenges, a number of technical and access issues have been addressed by the ELP including: the use of open source versus proprietary courseware; static and dynamic materials to be designed and delivered online; designing opportunities for student interaction; and the design, development and use of 'learning object' repositories.

C.   Open source management systems and access

As noted earlier, a variety of platforms are currently in use at AU. The ELP is engineering a move to encourage the development and use of open-source management systems rather than expanding the use of proprietary software. Students in the future will access all AU courses and materials through a portal system which will also be used to manage grade books and library, student service and registry functions. Students will also be encouraged to communicate with tutors, course professors and, with permission, other students via email.

D.   Static course materials

As noted earlier, a wide spectrum of approaches to online course development and delivery currently exists at AU. However, the ELP now defines a number of basic elements specifying what it means for a course to be labelled as an e-learning course. To begin with, all AU-produced materials - student manuals, study guides, lab manuals - will be online in addition to reading files, either through online reproduction where copyright permits, or through linking to AU's online journal databases. Although it is premature to talk about the actual inclusion of e-books in course materials, when they become available in formats that are workable for both faculty and students, they will also, where applicable, form part of the online course package. AU is currently collaborating with a company specialising in e-book development and distribution, as well as working on several pilot projects to evaluate the feasibility of using e-books as part of the online course materials package. Streamed audio and video components that do not violate copyright and that enhance teaching and learning will also be included. AU is discussing these options with a video production company and will shortly be piloting streamed video components in an introductory Spanish course.

E.   Dynamic course components

Tutor-student and faculty-student interaction in all courses will be enabled via e-mail. Students will also be provided with online access to all student services – counselling and registration for example - and each course will be linked to the library and a Digital Reading Resource tailored specifically to each individual course. Each course will also access a bank of frequently-asked-questions and course bulletin boards, enabling tutors to broadcast information and course updates. Online submission of assignments will be facilitated as will online marking of assignments. Quizzes and self-assessment tests will be delivered and marked online. Many of these online features are already available to students in a variety of AU's courses.

F.   Group interaction.

Proponents of e-learning suggest that in this environment, learning should be an active process and teaching should be interactive (Ellis and Phelps, 2000). Web-based teaching requires new and innovative approaches to the presentation of material, student-teacher dialogue, group interaction, and assessment. Some view online education as fundamentally a group communication phenomenon where "[c]onstructivism has become a synonym for learning by doing" (Harasim, 2000, 54). Online learning environments have been shown to provide students with a great learning advantage in the area of online conferencing. The development of meaningful online peer interaction situations presents special challenges to course delivery at AU. As noted earlier, courses offered in the individualised study mode, with continuous enrollments throughout twelve months of the year, account for 90% of AU's undergraduate registrations. Once students have registered in a course, their participation is self-paced. The only time constraint placed upon them is a six month contract period in which they are expected to complete their three-credit course, with some flexibility built in for extensions. Therefore, although there may be a group of students who each register in the same course at the same time, individual students are not moving through the course with a cohort of peers and this makes the development of meaningful interactive conferencing difficult. Students value the flexible start dates and the unpaced nature of AU's courses. Given the advantages that online delivery presents for the facilitation of peer-to-peer interaction, strategies are currently being explored to design these interactions while at the same time not detracting from the advantages of unpaced study.

G.   Learning Objects

The ELP also suggests that courses will be linked to appropriate learning objects at AU and elsewhere and that students will be able to access their learning resources from four general sources: course materials produced by AU; purchased texts and other media; the library; and external sources such as the Web, local libraries and so on. Educational content is increasingly being conceptualised and developed in a modular digital format known as 'learning objects'. These objects will be designed to be sequenced, contextualised and reused in a variety of educational applications as a strategy to effectively manage, use and reuse them. Management will be facilitated by tagging the objects and storing them in repositories where they can be searched, accessed and combined to create new learning sequences and courses. AU has recently received a federal government grant in excess of half a million Canadian dollars for facilitation of research, development of interoperable standards and specifications for educational modelling, object identification and rights management and for the development of implementation strategies for an effective learning object repository.

5.   Steps to Achieving E-Learning Plan Goals

In order to achieve these goals the ELP proposes the development of a suite of supported tools and systems that enable the implementation of the basic functions described above. These systems will integrate with all other AU systems as required (see Figure 1).

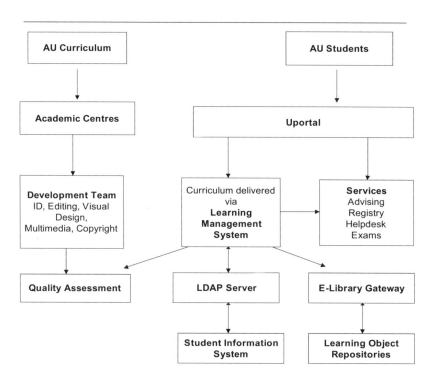

Figure 1.   Framework for the AU E-Learning System

In the interim, no new proprietary or other learning platforms will be introduced at AU. Current systems will be reviewed and adapted as necessary to implement the ELP vision. The current course production policy will be reviewed and amended to incorporate procedures and criteria for e-learning courses and adoption of XML-type languages to produce course materials that are, as far as possible, medium neutral. According to several online distance educators, the design of e-learning activities – like the design of educational multi-media products – benefits greatly from bringing together teams of individuals (faculty content experts, visual designers, multimedia designers, instructional Webspace designers and editors), each with their own unique skills (Bates, 2000; Care and Scanlan, 2001; Hughes and Hay, 2001; Kang, 2001). Although AU has always used a team approach to development of print-based materials, course development often occurred sequentially, with some looped-feedback in the process. Several online course development team projects are currently underway at AU. Policies and protocols will need to be developed to guide the tracking of online course versions, including a well documented archiving system.

6.   Challenges for the E-Learning Plan

As noted earlier, AU currently offers in excess of 500 undergraduate courses, most of which are delivered in print-based format. The systematic plan for online conversion of courses sees all new courses and major revisions developed for online delivery from January 2003. For some centres - Centre for Computing and Information Systems, Nursing and Health Studies, the undergraduate School of Business - where the course development process is largely decentralised, the conversion will be built into their rolling three-year business plans. The ELP sees all senior, discussion-based, reading, and project courses being developed or converted to an online format as appropriate. Over the next few years, high enrollment courses will be systematically reviewed with regard to their suitability and timing for online conversion.

Although the directives and the processes of the ELP have been well defined, there are issues and controversies surrounding online course conversions and development; these will require thoughtful consideration, exploration and evaluation as conversion unfolds. Notwithstanding obvious technical and financial constraints, the most critical issues to face are those related to the people of AU. Concerns about online course design, pedagogy, digital content and quality, workload, costs and benefits, access issues and research and evaluation are relevant and clearly will inform e-learning debates with students, faculty, tutors and staff in mind.

A.   Students

AU's primary concern in planning its e-learning initiatives and strategies are its students and its commitment to the removal of barriers restricting access to university studies. Various authors have made claims for the rising popularity of the Internet and for the increasing connectivity of students (ACOL, 2001; Kidwell et al, 2000). While access statistics, at least in North America, are impressive, having a computer and being able to connect to the Internet can not be equated to a desire to study online. For many students the shift to online learning environments can be quite disruptive and challenging, especially for those used to classroom environments (Essex and Cagiltay, 2001).

Typical of learners at other distance institutions, the majority of AU's students are employed (83%) and not surprisingly most (59%) face barriers to pursuing campus-based university education (Halsne and Gatta, 2002). These barriers most frequently include family and job responsibilities and the distance to a post-secondary institution. For students who choose to study at AU, almost all (95%) indicate that it is important that they were able to start courses any month of the year and that they are able to work at their own pace (97%). Over the past few years AU has seen a dramatic increase in the proportion of students who choose to contact their course tutors via e-mail rather than on the telephone. Ninety-four percent of non-computing students at AU have home computers that are less than three years old and the proportion with Internet connections is currently reported at 93%. Dial-in connections are still the most predominant but just over 25% of students were using cable modem connections in 2001. Approximately 71% of non-computing students indicated they would be interested in using a computer in their AU studies. Clearly, AU's students, at least its domestic population, are enthusiastic about the prospect of learning online.

AU recognises that information on the web is not always easy for students to reference. It is neither transportable nor tangible in the same way as are print-based materials. Findings indicate that students learning online continue to print web-based materials and some research suggests that the primary reason for doing so is to enable studying (Kaminski, 2001). The challenge for AU will be to provide learning environments that take advantage of online technologies. We know that network technologies can increase the speed with which we interact with students and can greatly enhance communications between students. Online technologies will enhance AU's capacity to provide a variety of support and administrative services more conveniently for students. Furthermore, it is becoming increasingly important for all learners to be able to use technology to study, interact with others, and research information from digital resources.

B.   Faculty, Tutors, and Staff

The ELP recognises that academics will play the central role in the conception, design and delivery of e-courses. Academic staff - faculty, course co-ordinators and tutors - at AU share many of the concerns expressed by others making the transition, either from classroom based teaching or distance delivery education to online teaching. Part of faculty stress arises from the challenges of learning about the new technologies and trying to understand how these technologies will fit with existing and new pedagogies. However, some of this stress is a function of increases in workload. Although AU faculty are already familiar with the increased demands on time that planning and preparing distance education courses requires, designing e-courses is time consuming, at least during transition periods, and can potentially impact on faculty's ability to fulfil other scholarly activities (McAlister et al, 2001). As the shift to online course delivery unfolds, faculty responsibilities and workloads will undoubtedly change (Wallhaus, 2000).

Faculty and tutors will require a variety of supports and training as courses are developed, converted or enhanced, and this has been built into ELP (Ellis and Phelps, 2000). AU has the advantage, as a longstanding distance education provider, of being able to provide the necessary support and training to faculty. EMD currently employs five multimedia instructional designers as well as three visual designers. Once academic centres have established their 3-year operational plans - to include e-learning adoption or enhancements - a needs analysis by centre can be undertaken and appropriate training and support provided (either through centre-based systems or through AU departments such as Computing Services and EMD). New academic staff will be expected to be adept in basic computer use, online systems and online course development and delivery.

Given the goals set by the SUP, it is clear that the tutoring role will continue to evolve at AU and a key success factor will be AU's ability to recruit, train (or re-train) and support those who tutor in a predominantly online environment. AU has considerable experience and expertise in this area but the lack of coherence in e-learning has hindered a more coordinated approach to these issues. An outcome of this ELP will be to establish, with appropriate representation from employee groups, a working group to plan for the impact of e-learning on the faculty, tutors and staff.

C.   Training

Forty percent of higher education institutions provide no information technology training to faculty (Care and Scanlan, 2001). The training plan to support this ELP is to be guided by the general principle that academics and tutors must be familiar with and knowledgeable about all aspects of the course and the other services available to students. The training plan also assumes that all academics and tutors have basic computer skills and those responsible for the development and maintenance of these materials must be highly computer literate. The development of detailed training objectives and the implementation of the plan will be driven by the organisational structures in place to support this plan and, in particular, whether academics, tutors and coordinators are doing much of the work themselves or need adequate support and professional staff to develop, maintain and sustain the online resources. Training resources will be offered online where possible to afford the most flexibility in time and place. Where such flexibility is not possible, training materials and events will be developed that will facilitate achieving the training objective. Evaluation of the training plan will be based on demonstration of the skills learned rather than on numbers participating in training.

D.   Technology

Throughout the conversion process the impact that broadband, multi-media and wireless systems have on course development, delivery and, most importantly, student access will be under constant consideration and evaluation.

E.   Digital Content and Quality/Cost-Benefits

It is clear that e-learning will create new categories of costs and/or shift the relative importance of certain costs within institutions (Bates, 2000; Wallhaus, 2000). Others have noted how little evaluation universities do of their spending on information technology and that they cannot identify the actual costs associated with online course development (Green, 2001). Harasim indicates a cost of 15 million Canadian Dollars to build a full programme for 2000 students (Harasim, 2000). Jesshope suggests 200 hours of preparation time for every hour of online delivery (Jesshope, 2001). Major challenges to the course design and delivery process will include assessments of time and costs along with flexibility in re-allocation of resources (Kang, 2001).

F.   Research and Evaluation

As a research and teaching university, AU is committed both to engaging in research that pursues and creates new knowledge and to viewing all of our instructional activities within a scholarly framework. To this end, the challenge will be to actively investigate, reflect upon and disseminate the results of our continuous innovations in teaching and learning. As a learning organisation we are committed to providing continuous opportunities for our staff and our students to acquire new skills and knowledge and to share these resources within a learning community. The development of e-learning provides both opportunity and obligation for AU to enhance its instructional research and evaluation efforts. Each academic and student service centre will be encouraged to develop a teaching, learning and evaluation plan and to identify the specific research questions most important to the development of e-learning within its disciplinary/service context. Lead by the Institute for Research on Open and Distance Learning, funding will be secured to pursue this research agenda and to disseminate the results.

7.   Conclusions

In order to ensure the most effective processes and outcomes possible, AU will take a leadership role in developing and implementing benchmarks that gauge its progress in developing quality e-learning. The university will work with established standards and will explore opportunities to work with other universities in benchmarking activities. In addition, research into aspects of student attitudes regarding access to, and needs for, communication technologies for learning and for active and effective participation in modern society will be undertaken. Related to this, mission critical data related to enrollments, completion and attrition rates, the needs of special groups of students and the effectiveness of AU's delivery techniques and technologies will be monitored, reported and assessed on a regular basis.

Clearly, the shift proposed in this ELP has to occur with the needs of each course and learners in mind, especially with regard to course materials. The development of guidelines and policies, the use of pilot studies, the evaluation of the effectiveness of various practices, and ongoing debate about e-learning will be needed, especially with respect to pedagogy. In any shift from print to online media, the pedagogical intent of a course needs to be preserved or recreated, and this will demand the coaching of the course team members in the pedagogical possibilities of the new medium. Various authors have suggested a need for new instructional theories to guide the effective use of online learning technologies, claiming that existing instructional design models and theories are incapable of prescribing conditions for interactive learning offered by multi- and hyper-media systems (Mann, 2000b). Although AU currently considers itself as an online institution, the ELP proposes a shift from the current undergraduate course development system, based on individualised study using print materials, telephone and e-mail tutoring and optional online derivatives, to one that regards the online learning environment as primary, and designs course materials, learning activities and tutoring models with that in mind. An important dimension of the ELP is to initiate research into aspects of students' attitudes towards communication technologies for learning and their active and effective participation in modern society. AU students confront diverse and complex barriers to the acquisition of appropriate technology and connectivity. With AU's commitment to serve those traditionally under-served by higher education, the university will play a leadership role in the debate regarding the 'digital divide' that will inform not only its practices but the wider debate as well.

References

Abrioux, D. (2001a), 'Athabasca University, 1970 -2001: An historical perspective,' *Lunch 'n Learn Presentation*. Athabasca: Athabasca University.

Abrioux, D. (2001b), 'Strategic University Plan development and approval process', *Unpublished Manuscript*, Athabasca University.

Advisory Committee for Online Learning (AC0L) (2001), *The e-learning e-volution in colleges and universities.* Ottawa: Communications Branch Industry Canada. Available at http://www.schoolnet.ca/mlg/sites/acol-ccael (Accessed 15 December 2002).

Athabasca University (AU) (2002). *Strategic University Plan: 2002-2006.* Available at http://www.athabascau.ca/sup/sup_19_06.pdf (Accessed 15 December 2002)

Bates, A. (2000), *Managing technological change: Strategies for college and university leaders.* San Francisco: Jossey-Bass Publishers.

Berg, G. (1998), 'Public policy on distance learning in higher education: California State and Western Governors Association initiatives', *Education policy analysis archives.* 6: 1-15. Available at http://olam.ed.asu.edu/epaa/v6n11.html (Accessed 15 December 2002).

Bower, B. (2001), 'Distance education: facing the faculty challenge', *Journal of distance learning administration.* 4(2) . Available at http://www.westga.edu/~distance/ojdla/summer42/bower42.html (Accessed 15 December 2002).

Burniske, R. and Monke, L., (2001), *Breaking Down the Digital Walls: Learning to Teach in a Post-Modem World.* Albany: State University of New York Press.

Care, W. and Scanlan, J. (2001), 'Planning and managing the development of courses for distance delivery: Results from a qualitative study', *Journal of distance learning administration,* 4(2). Available at http://www.westga.edu/~distance/ojdla/summer42/care42.html (Accessed 15 December 2002).

Edelstein, S. and Edwards, J. (2002), 'If you build it, they will come: Building learning communities through threaded discussions', *Journal of distance learning administration,* 5(1). Available at http://www.westga.edu/%7distance/ojdla/spring51/edelstein51.html (Accessed 15 December 2002).

Ellis, A. and Phelps, R. (2000), 'Managing staff development for web-based teaching: A four-stage model and its application', in: B. Mann (ed.)

Perspectives in Web course management. Toronto: Canadian Scholars' Press: 35-50.

Essex, C. and Cagiltay, K. (2001), 'Evaluating an online course: Feedback from "distressed" students', *The quarterly review of distance education,* 2: 233 - 239.

Gerson, S. (2000), 'E-CLASS: Creating a guide to online course development for distance learning faculty', *Online journal of distance learning administration,* 3(4), Available at http://www.westga.edu/~distance/ojdla/winter34/gerson34.html (Accessed 15 December 2002).

Gibbons, H. and Wentworth, G. (2001), 'Andrological and pedagogical training differences for online instructors', *Online journal of distance learning administration,* 4(3). Available at http://www.westga.edu/~distance/ojdla/fall43/gibbons_wentworth43.html (Accessed 15 December 2002).

Gordon, O. (2000), 'Pedagogical issues in Internet education', *Perspectives,* 3: 1-6.

Green, M. (2001), *By his contrivance - a theoretical perspective of delivering technology in higher education,* Round Table No. 8 (May 1998) Seams in the Seamless: Technology and Delivery. The Australian National University. Available at http://www.asap.unimelb.edu.au/nscf/roundtables/roundtable_8_green.htm (Accessed 15 December 2002).

Halsne, A. and Gatta, L. (2002), 'Online versus traditionally-delivered instruction: A descriptive study of learner characteristics in a community college setting', *Online journal of distance learning administration,* 5(1). Available at http://www.westga.edu/%7Edistance/ojdla/spring51/halsne51.html (Accessed 15 December 2002).

Harasim, L. (2000), 'Shift happens: Online education as a new paradigm in learning', *The Internet and higher education,* 3: 41 - 61.

Hughes, G. and Hay, D. (2001), 'Use of concept mapping to integrate the different perspectives of designers and other stakeholders in the development of e-learning materials', *British journal of educational technology,* 32: 557 - 569.

Jesshope, C. (2001), 'Cost-effective multimedia in on-line teaching', *Educational technology and society*, 4(3). Available at http://ifets.ieee.org/periodical/vol_3_2001/jesshope.html   (Accessed   15 December 2002).

Johnson, J. and DeSpain, B. (2001), 'Policies and practices in the utilization of interactive television and web-based delivery models in public universities', *Online journal of distance learning administration*, 4(2): 1-16. Available at http://www.westga.edu/~distance/ojdla/summer42/johnson42.htm (Accessed 15 December 2002).

Kaminski, K. (2001), 'The effect of printing on satisfaction with Web-based instruction', *The quarterly review of distance education*, 2: 241 - 246.

Kang, S. (2001), 'Toward a collaborative model for the design of Web-based courses', *Educational technology*, March-April 2001: 22 - 30.

Katz, R. (2000), 'Information policy to support campus e-business', in: R. Katz and D. Oblinger (eds.) *The "e" is for everything: E-commerce, e-business, and e-learning in higher education (Educause, Leadership strategies no. 2)*. San Francisco: Jossey Bass. 71 - 86.

Kidwell, J., Mattie, J. and Sousa, M. (2000), 'Preparing your campus for e-business', in R. Katz and D. Oblinger (eds.) *The "e" is for everything: E-commerce, e-business, and e-learning in higher education (Educause, Leadership strategies no. 2)*. San Francisco: Jossey Bass, 87 - 113.

MacDonald, J. (2001), 'Exploiting online interactivity to enhance assignment development and feedback in distance education', *Open learning*, 16: 179 - 189.

Mann, B. (2000a), Preface in B. Mann (ed.) *Perspectives in Web course management*. Toronto: Canadian Scholars' Press, vii - xi.

Mann, B. (2000b), 'Phase theory: A teleological taxonomy of Web course management', in B. Mann (ed.) *Perspectives in Web course management*. Toronto: Canadian Scholars' Press, 3 – 25

McAlister, M., Rivera, J. and Hallam, S. (2001), 'Twelve important questions to answer before you offer a Web-based curriculum', *Journal of distance learning administration*, 4(2). Available at

http://www.westga.edu/~distance/ojdla/summer42/mcalister42.html
(Accessed 15 December 2002).

Noble, D. (1997), *Digital diploma mills, Part I: The automation of higher education.* Available at http://www.communication.ucsd.edu/dl/ddm1.html (Accessed 15 December 2002).

Noble, D. (1998a), *Digital diploma mills, Part II: The coming battle over online instruction.* Available at http://www.communication.ucsd.edu/dl/ddm2.html   (Accessed   15 December 2002).

Noble, D. (1998b), *Digital diploma mills, Part III: The bloom is off the rose.* Available at http://www.communication.ucsd.edu/dl/ddm3.html   (Accessed   15 December 2002).

Noble, D. (1999), *Digital diploma mills, Part IV: Rehearsal for the revolution.* Available at http://www.communication.ucsd.edu/dl/ddm4.html   (Accessed   15 December 2002).

Oblinger, D. and Katz, R. (2000), 'Navigating the sea of 'e'', in R. Katz and D. Oblinger (eds.) *The "e" is for everything: E-commerce, e-business, and e-learning in higher education (Educause, Leadership strategies No. 2).* San Francisco: Jossey Bass, 1-10.

Palloff, R. and Pratt, K. (1999), B*uilding learning communities in cyberspace: Effective strategies for the online classroom.* San Francisco: Josey-Bass Publishers.

Rahman, M. (2001), 'Faculty recruitments strategies for online programs', *Journal of distance learning administration,* 4(4). Available at http://www.westga.edu/~distance/ojdla/winter44/rahman44.html (Accessed 15 December 2002).

Wallhaus, R. (2000), 'E-Learning: From institutions to providers, from students to learners', in R. Katz and D. Oblinger (eds.) *The "e" is for everything: E-commerce, e-business, and e-learning in higher education (Educause, Leadership strategies No. 2).* San Francisco: Jossey Bass, 21 - 52.

Western Interstate Commission for Higher Education (WICHE) (2002), *The cooperative advancing the effective use of technology in higher education*. Available at http://www.edutools.info/course/index.jsp (Accessed 15 December 2002).

Yeung, D. (2002), 'Toward an effective quality assurance model of Web-based learning: The perspective of academic staff', *Journal of distance learning administration,* 5(2). Available at http://www.westgau.edu/~distance/ojdla/summer52/yeung52.html (Accessed 15 December 2002).

Online Resource Page:
Using Technology to Enhance Online Interactivity

Brent Muirhead

Abstract

Today's online administrators and instructors are investigating ways to foster a dynamic learning environment. Currently "Internet technology empowers the joint exploration of the delivery mechanisms of previous generations, adding stronger collaborative learning elements" (Passerini and Granger, 2000, 3). Contemporary Internet technologies are helping remove the idea of distance from online education. The online teaching and learning process could produce more relevant and consistent interaction than that produced in traditional undergraduate classrooms. A large traditional classroom does create communication barriers that make it difficult for all students to participate in class discussions. It is interesting that university students are using emails more often to share with their classmates and teachers. The Internet is providing a practical way to remove learning barriers and encourage greater access to intellectual resources. The idea of distance education has fostered the pursuit of new educational paradigms that encourage online education to be more personal and student-centered. The potential instructional advantages and challenges associated with the Resource Page, a new web-based tool created for online teachers at the University of Phoenix, will be highlighted.

1.   Contemporary Distance Education Challenges

A major concern among academic officials has often focused on the quality of educational experiences within an online class. Carnevale relates that research studies indicate that the essential features of a good course include "interaction between instructors and students, a student-centered approach and built-in opportunities for students to learn on their own" (Carnevale, 2000, A46). Creating and sustaining a quality online degree program is a challenging venture. There are a variety of factors that can have either a positive or negative impact on the online educational setting:

- the level of expertise of the online faculty (technical and online experience)
- the degree of administrative financial support
- the technological infrastructure of the school
- the student support system to handle academic and computer-related issues
- the depth and quality of faculty training and professional development programs

(Cooper, 2000).

Contemporary online instructors must continually upgrade their courses to help prepare students for current and future jobs and educational opportunities. Nichols highlights six imperatives for educators in the 21st Century:

- Increased capacity and efficiency - through enabling institutions to cater for the learning of a relatively large number of students at once
- Improved effectiveness - by encouraging deep learning approaches and the adaptation of knowledge to the real world
- Easy accessibility - by removing distance barriers and catering for a variety of learners' prior educational experience, physical abilities and time commitments/lifestyles
- A competitive mindset - education with the potential to be offered internationally, within industry and at a distance, providing more choice and convenience for the student
- A resource-based emphasis - enabling more student control over what, where, when and how they study and permitting non-linear learning
- The personal touch - with more interaction between students and between individual student and tutor, enabling a degree of customization and the pursuit of individual students' learning goals in addition to the prescribed course learning outcomes

(Nichols, 2001, 13-14).

2.   UOP Background and Educational Philosophy

The University of Phoenix (UOP) is recognized as a leader in adult education. The institution was established in 1976 and was accredited in 1978 by the Higher Learning Commission of the North Central Association. The institution serves a student population of 164,700 students who are involved in traditional or face-to-face and online classes. The consolidated enrolment of its educational programs makes it the largest private higher education school in the United States (Apollo Group, 2002). Students can attend classes online and on-campus at 121 campuses that are located in 25 US states, Canada and Puerto Rico. The average student age is 34 years old, 54% are female and 46% are male, and the average household income is $50,000-$60,000 (University of Phoenix, 2002b).

John Sperling, who was educated at Cambridge University, was the founder of the University of Phoenix. During the early 1970s, Sperling conducted adult education research projects as a professor at San Jose State University in San Jose, California. The research studies investigated educational delivery systems that effectively met the needs of adult students. Sperling was concerned that traditional residential universities were neglecting their adult students. Sperling's research affirmed the importance of having education programs that are adult-centered and sensitive to adults' unique learning needs. He proposed an educational model that focused on adult learners through innovative and student-centered program design, curriculum, teaching methods and student services (Swenson, 2001).

The for-profit institution has created a creative and flexible educational model based on the following principles:

- To facilitate cognitive and affective student learning - knowledge, skills and values - and to promote use of that knowledge in the students' workplaces
- To develop competence in communication, critical thinking, collaboration, and information utilisation, together with a commitment to lifelong learning for enhancement of students' opportunities for career success
- To provide instruction that bridges the gap between theory and practice through faculty members who bring to their classrooms not only advanced academic preparation, but also the skills that come from the current practice of their professions
- To use technology to create effective modes and means of instruction that expand access to learning resources and that enhance collaboration and communication for improved student learning
- To assess student learning and use assessment data to improve the teaching/learning system, curriculum, instruction, learning resources, counseling and student services
- To be organized as a for-profit institution in order to foster a spirit of innovation that focuses on providing academic quality, service, excellence and convenience to the working adult
- To generate the financial resources necessary to support the University's mission

(Swenson, 2001, 3-4).

The school strives to maintain a relatively small full-time staff to run their educational services. A core of 285 full-time faculty members provide essential leadership by establishing academic standards and supervising curriculum development. In addition, approximately 17,000 adjunct teachers (part-time staff) who are actively engaged in the teaching and research of their subjects and disciplines are utilised in facilitating students' learning (University of Phoenix, 2003a). This facilitator model is based on rigorous academic standards and expectations, requiring educators who are capable of equipping students to be independent learners.

Prospective faculty must successfully complete a training class and mentorship before they become faculty members. Faculty candidates at UOP receive four weeks of training prior to their mentorship. The class provides extensive opportunities for individuals to become familiar with Microsoft's Outlook Express software program that is used for the online classes. The candidates learn about the essence of computer-mediated education by reading relevant lectures, responding to weekly questions and online scenarios, working on team projects, studying UOP academic policies and observing online classes. It is an intensive training format but candidates appreciate their trainers who share guidance and insights on the teaching and learning process. The class is an essential component in equipping individuals with the basic knowledge and skills to facilitate their first online class.

Why does the University of Phoenix place so much emphasis on training their new faculty? Research studies reveal that the quality of online education classes varies considerably due to instructors who fail to provide timely and consistent feedback to their students (Caudron, 2001; Muirhead, 1999). UOP has created a dynamic training and mentoring process that is designed to help instructors make the transition from the traditional classroom setting to becoming effective online instructors. The university wants to make sure that instructors are well prepared to facilitate online classes. Then, more students will have positive online educational experiences.

The need for training is highlighted by the diversity of tasks that are expected of online instructors. For instance, instructors at UOP will facilitate learning teams in their classes. Moderating the group process requires having the knowledge and skills to effectively promote successful collaboration. Guiding the learning teams requires knowing how to create a setting that engages all participants in sharing online and completing a variety of projects. Collison et al have listed eight instructor tasks that must be performed to foster dynamic small groups:

- Leading introductory, community-building activities
- Providing virtual 'hand-holding' to the 'digitally challenged'
- Acknowledging the diversity of participants' backgrounds and interests
- Infusing personality with tone, graphics and humour
- Maintaining a nurturing pace of responding
- Keeping up with the pace set
- Organising posts and discussion threads
- Balancing private email and public discussion

(Collison et al, 2000, 49).

The University of Phoenix takes a student-centered approach when developing degree programs by making them accessible to working adults. The traditional face-to-face classes are offered during the evenings and weekends. The online classes can be accessed through the Internet at any time during the day or night. Classes are usually five to six weeks in length and students normally take one class at a time. UOP offers a diversity of degree programs: associate, bachelor, master, and doctoral. The University places a priority on designing institutional goals, programs and services that are sensitive to adult learning characteristics and needs. Students are encouraged to obtain the skills and knowledge to be leaders at work and in their communities.

3. Resource Page Overview

A challenging problem for distance education systems is how to provide a large number of students across diverse geographical areas with consistent materials and resources that will ultimately allow them to achieve their personal and professional goals. This will require a change in the way technology is used in schools (Grabe, 1998). In order to address this problem, the University of Phoenix has eliminated the need for all hard-copy materials by developing an online 'resource page' for students and faculty. Instead of buying a textbook at the beginning of a course, students will pay a resource access fee that will make available their learning resources for each course. Ultimately, the small access fees will save students money because they will not have to purchase expensive textbooks. The computer technology requirements for using the resource page are quite basic so the resource page is available to students who possess either a modem, DSL or cable modem connection to the Internet.

In recognition of the fact that all students have unique learning styles, the University of Phoenix Online has begun the implementation process of the Resource Page that will be integrated into the online curriculum. The Resource Page is a dynamic product that will greatly improve the delivery of student and faculty materials. The product is a set of learning tools that are designed and presented in a variety of modalities in order to meet the needs of all learners. These materials will be delivered via the Student and Faculty Web on a course-by-course basis. To facilitate this strategic initiative, the university is partnering with a variety of publishers to provide content and other ancillary services. UOP currently has partnership arrangements with Thomson Learning, Pearson Publishing, McGraw Hill, Course Technology and John Wiley.

The resource page is not only an 'e-book'; it is a collection of electronically delivered learning resources (one element of which is an 'e-text') which are closely aligned to the course objectives. These collections can be differentiated as visual databases, multimedia libraries and more

(Barron, 1994). For example, instead of a textbook with perhaps 20 chapters from which reading assignments would be chosen for assigned reading, the instructor can assign the specific portions of the e-text of their resource page to correspond with the number of class meetings or workshops and the material will relate specifically to the learning objectives. PowerPoint presentations that correspond to the course objectives, as well as self-assessments, multimedia activities and current articles from the digital library will be available. This allows each faculty member to maintain a more distinct focus on course or workshop objectives. Additionally, students will have access to their entire 'reference library' of university materials from their desktop or laptop and will be able to access their library (with automatic updates) as alumni.

4.   Resource Page: Detailed Descriptions
University of Phoenix courses will contain the following materials as part of this new initiative:

A.   UniModule
The UniModule is the recommended curriculum for a given course; it is developed in a format that provides course guidance for instructional training, whether conducted in the classroom, online or in a directed study format. This document contains course topics, objectives and assignments, as well as a content outline for instructors. Faculty members have the flexibility to make modifications to the curriculum, as long as they adequately address specific course objectives as outlined in the UniModule. In doing so, the University ensures that course content is consistently delivered to students across all campuses.

B.   E-Text
The e-text is the selected 'textbook' for each course. In some cases, this material is simply an electronic copy of an existing textbook; in other cases, the e-text is a compilation of material from multiple sources including chapters from several textbooks, associated selected readings and other printed materials. Students view this material using Microsoft® Reader or by printing all or part of the text from their personal computers.

C.   Supplemental Materials
Information contained in this link will vary from course to course. It may contain course-specific PowerPoint presentations, program specific guides (i.e. APA reference information), assessment tools, case studies, unique learning activities, topic-specific tutorials, video clips and computer simulations.

D.   Articles

Each course comes with a set of selected readings, which are a compilation of journal articles and other scholarly literature from the University's Online Collection. These articles have been specially selected by course developers to supplement the readings in the e-text and to further ensure students are prepared to meet the course objectives.

E.   Internet Resources

Each course will also have 2-5 associated web links that will direct students to areas on the web that will further enhance their professional development. Typically, students will explore the sites of professional associations, other related organisations and sites that encourage professional collaboration and/or community involvement. For instance, teachers and students in the educational programs have access to relevant journals and publications such as *Phi Delta Kappan* and *Education World.*

F.   Multimedia

The University has partnered with several companies to allow students to develop ancillary skills that will further facilitate their learning. In this section, students are provided with a variety of tutorials, from novice to advanced levels, designed to enhance their technological and professional skills. Examples of online tutorials available to students are: Windows, Word, PowerPoint and Access Excel.

The school has invested significant financial resources into developing relevant computer simulations for their online classes. UOP has created practical simulations that are narrated and interactive. For instance, graduate education faculty will have access to over 100 simulations that they can use in their classes.

5.   Services
A.   University Library

The Online Collection, the most popular part of the Library website contains databases with millions of full text articles, documents, reference sources, directories and financial data. Students may use the Online Collection to obtain direct access to subscription resources not normally found through Internet search engines. In addition to the subscription databases in the Online Collection, there are also many helpful websites for research available at no cost on the World Wide Web.

B.   Writing Lab

The University of Phoenix operates a virtual writing lab, known as the Center for Writing Excellence, and its services are freely offered to all students. The 'lab' is actually an email address where students can send their written materials (papers, projects and so on) to be reviewed by qualified University of Phoenix faculty members and receive feedback. The lab is not an editing service and faculty will not revise student papers. Instead, experienced writing instructors will review work and give detailed feedback on how to improve specific papers and on writing style in general. Feedback will focus on format, grammar, organisation, punctuation and usage, but not course content. Instructors continue to provide content-oriented feedback in their assessment of student papers and projects.

It usually takes approximately 48 hours for the writing lab staff to review a paper and return it to students. Students appreciate the detailed and timely feedback on their work. Additionally, student learning team papers can be submitted for review. Currently, the writing lab is receiving over 4,000 papers a month from students seeking assistance.

Students can access the web-based portion of the writing lab for guidance on a variety of writing issues. It contains interactive tutorials, writing samples and the MLA, APA and UOP writing style guides.

C.   Proficiency Assessments

The Skills Enhancement Center contains math, critical thinking and English tutorials. Each tutorial contains instructional material, learning questions, quizzes and practice exams. This material will assist students in preparing for their proficiency exams.

The Testing Center contains the official math, critical thinking and English proficiency exams. Students are required to take one or more of these assessments, depending on specific program requirements. Tests are available online and students receive immediate feedback upon completion of the exams.

6.   Program-Specific Resources
A.   Program Handbook

Program handbooks contain program-specific information for students, including program sequence, course descriptions and graduation requirements. This 'virtual' document replaces the traditional hard-copy books previously supplied to students upon enrollment.

B.   Downloads

This section provides students with free downloads for the following resources:
- Microsoft® Reader
- Adobe® Acrobat® Reader®
- Internet Explorer

C.   Electronic Portfolio (Education Programs)
This is a link to the students' individual web-based electronic portfolios. The document represents a teacher's continuous progress and development throughout their program and career. Elements of the portfolio are designed to ensure that students meet state, national, and program standards and are evaluated using formative and summative methods. This tool is introduced during the first course and reinforced by faculty in each course.
Teachers also post their Teacher Work Sample Project in this portfolio. This project is a 4 week, standards-based unit that include the following elements:
- Unit learning goals
- Contextual information
- Content
- Assessment plan
- Pre-assessment analysis
- Design for instruction
- Descriptions of two featured students
- The instructional process of the two featured students
- Analysis of learning results
- Reflection on teaching and learning

7.   Teacher Preparation Accountability
A.   Benefits of the Resource Page
This Resource Page can encourage teachers to more consistently display the following practices in their online classes:
- Support students' acquisition of substantive learning by designing units of instruction that employ a range of strategies that build on each students' strengths, needs and prior experiences
- Align learning goals with state and district content standards
- Adjust the classroom environment and instruction to address important contextual characteristics of the classroom
- Employ a variety of instructional resources to help students attain learning goals and to offer them new opportunities to explore important ideas or to learn new skills that have relevance to their lives
- Use multiple assessment methods that appropriately measure learning gains towards the selected goals
- Explore students' understanding and thinking processes while evaluating the effectiveness of their teaching
- Analyse student learning by examining individual, small group, and whole class achievement

- Use their analysis of student assessment to guide instruction, to provide feedback to students and to plan for professional development
- Provide credible evidence of their instructional effectiveness through student performance

(Pokay et al, 2001).

B.   Disadvantages of the Resource Page

What are some of the concerns and observations about the resource page?

- There is debate among educators and academic publishers continues over the educational effectiveness of using e-books, particularly concerning access issues. There is resistance to using digital books and some students prefer having print textbooks. Mayfield voices concerns that students will be reluctant to use their computers to read for extended periods of time (Mayfield, 2001).
- There is doubt over whether the resource page design will help stimulate relevant interaction with the course material and with other learners.
- Instructional design issues involving the costs involved in creating an educational setting to effectively use the resource page.
- The importance of having qualified online instructors who can effectively implement new technology-based teaching strategies must be recognised.
- There is a need for more research and the willingness of innovators to listen and learn from constructive criticism of their work to encourage academic collaboration and improve online instructional resources.

8.   Challenges for Today's Online Instructors

The goal of this new initiative is to enhance the online teaching and learning process. It is designed to be a place that will provide instructional resources for a variety of educational needs. For instance, the resource page has foundational articles that are tied to the course objectives, yet instructors have the freedom to use their subject expertise to add articles and other instructional resources for their students. Perhaps it is better to view the resource page as a fluid document that has foundational materials but it is much more than just a set of e-books.

A brief study of the Reource Page highlights the importance of having trained teachers who are effective at facilitating online classes. It is vital that today's online instructors possess expertise in academic content areas and have the interpersonal skills that enable them to work with a diversity of students. An effective facilitator will be able to create a friendly and intellectually challenging class that has lively dialogue and relevant assignments that reflect high academic standards. The University continues to foster professional growth in their new and veteran faculty members through online workshops and regular peer reviews of their online classes.

Distance education literature contains frequent references to the importance of critical thinking and teachers are encouraged to cultivate reflective thought in their students. Yet, even veteran teachers will admit that integrating critical thinking instruction into their classes is one of their most difficult tasks. Teachers who want to enhance the teaching and learning process realise that fostering critical thinking skills will require extra work to effectively communicate complex ideas to their students. Bullen's research reveals that a student's ability to demonstrate critical thinking skills during online discussions is influenced by four major factors:

- cognitive maturity
- teaching style of instructor
- prior learning experiences
- degree of understanding of the critical thinking process (Bullen, 1998).

The list of factors reveals that students will vary in their understanding of critical thinking skills and cognitive abilities. Therefore, teachers will need to develop a set of strategies that will help them to meet a diversity of student needs.

Distance educators are challenged by using a text-driven form of education. Today's online classes rely heavily on printed materials and teacher-created lectures and handouts. Teachers can integrate critical thinking into their classes by presenting information from a diversity of perspectives that involve both the cognitive and affective learning domains. The Resource Page provides distance educators with a variety of instructional tools to stimulate higher-order thinking in their students. Obviously, teachers will need to customise some of the materials to meet specific learning objectives. However, the resource page represents a promising development in online education by emphasising the importance of having multidimensional teaching strategies, assignments and exercises.

The Resource Page will offer data for faculty, administration and accrediting organisations with an opportunity to regularly evaluate student performance and examine program effectiveness (D'Ignazio, 1996). Instructors can monitor student achievement to ensure that the course materials are closely aligned with the course objectives. A variety of resources will promote individualised instruction for a diversity of student learning styles and will encourage optimal learning experiences.

The resource page provides teachers with instructional resources that can help them promote deeper learning experiences. Instructors can offer supplementary materials that will enable them to meet the needs of students who possess different learning styles. Ultimately, online educators still hold the keys to making the online experience enjoyable for students. Spitzer notes "the missing link in Rosset's DL experience was not the technology, but the lack of a human mediator who could provide the things that technology could not: relevance, personalization, responsiveness, and flexibility" (Spitzer, 2001, 51-52). Research studies into interactivity in graduate education schools reveal that students want timely and consistent feedback. Students want personal attention from their instructors. It takes dedicated and effective facilitators that are frequently online to meet student needs. Traditional teachers sometimes have difficulty making the transition to working in the online environment. Being a good facilitator is a very challenging job and it is often far more demanding than traditional teaching (Muirhead, 2001).

The resource page offers students a variety of learning options that can individualise their educational experiences and make them more relevant. The student-centered model of learning encourages teachers to view their students as academic partners who work together to produce relevant and meaningful learning experiences. It requires educators who are willing to change their standard teaching methods. "[Educators] will need to become researchers of student perceptions, designers of multifaceted assessment strategies, managers of assessment processes and consultants assisting students in the interpretation of rich information about their learning" (Boud, 1995, 42).

Distance educators can evaluate their performance in online work by the extent to which they exhibit the following behaviours:

- Interacts on a regular basis in the online class
- Provides a detailed syllabus and weekly instructional updates on class work
- Writes messages that are clear, formatted properly and reflect appropriate spelling and grammar
- Uses personal and professional examples to stimulate discussion
- Writes with a good online tone (friendly, polite and professional)
- Interacts effectively with a diversity of students and works with lurkers

- Responds to student questions in a timely and consistent manner
- Demonstrates excitement/enthusiasm about the teaching and learning process
- Monitors student learning groups and encourages collaboration
- Builds upon student comments in a constructive way and uses creative prompts when necessary (for example, posts additional questions to help sustain and energize dialogue)
- Keeps the class focused on discussion questions and assignments
- Provides timely and consistent feedback by carefully explaining grades and offering specific, detailed and constructive comments on papers

(Muirhead et al, 2001, 6-7).

9.   Conclusion

The discussion of the resource page reveals the need for distance education schools to carefully select and train instructors for their online classes. It requires having qualified instructors who have the skills and knowledge expertise to effectively use the resource page. The University of Phoenix realises that it is a creative initiative that will require taking the time to experiment with teachers and students. The university is using conferences and Internet discussions as vital opportunities to obtain feedback to improve the resource page. For instance, students might want to have the option to use both textbooks and e-books in their classes. In the future, the school hopes to share a prototype for those interested in using the resource page for their organisations.

The creation of the electronic resource page is intended to foster a dynamic learning climate. It ensures that students will have access to more diverse and numerous information resources. Online instructors can ensure that students have access to the same materials that are tailored to specific course objectives. Teachers can use their subject knowledge expertise to creatively add materials such as PowerPoint presentations or video streams. The Resource Page has the potential to offer numerous instructional opportunities that will individualise online learning and promote rich educational experiences for today's students.

References

Apollo Group, (2002), *Investor Fact Sheet, August 2002*. Apollo Group Inc. http://www.apollogrp.edu/Investor_Relations/factsht.pdf (Accessed 7 April 2003).

Baron, A., Breit, F., Boulware, A. and Bullock, J. (1994), *Videodiscs in education: Overview, evaluation, activities*, 2nd ed. Tampa, FL: University of South Florida.

Boud, D. (1995), 'Assessment and learning: Contradictory or complimentary?', in: Knight, P. (ed.) *Assessment for learning in higher education.* London: Kogan. 35-48.

Bullen, M. (1998). 'Participation and critical thinking in online university distance education', *Journal of distance education.* 13(2). http://cade.icaap.org/vol13.2/bullen.html (accessed 7 April 2003).

Carnevale, D. (2000), 'Study assesses what participants look for in high-quality online courses', *Chronicle of higher education.* 47(9): A46.

Caudron, S. (2001), 'Evaluating e-degrees', *Workforce.* 80(2), 44-47.

Collison, G., Elbaum, B., Haavind, S. and Tinker, R. (2000), *Facilitating online learning: Effective strategies for moderators.* Madison, WI: Atwood.

Cooper, L. (2000), 'Online courses', *THE journal.* 27(8): 86-92.

D'Ignazio, F. (1996), 'Restructuring knowledge: Opportunities for classroom learning in the 1990s', *Computing teacher.* 18(1): 22-25.

Grabe, M. and Grabe, C. (1998), *Integrating technology for meaningful learning.* Boston, MA: Houghton Mifflin.

Mayfield, K. (2001), 'E-textbooks offer light reading', *Wired News.* http://www.wired.com/news/school/0,1383,45860,00.html (accessed on 7 April 2003).

Muirhead, B., McAuliffe, J. and La Rue, M. (2001), 'Online Resource Page: Using technology to enhance the teaching and learning process', *EducationaltTechnology and society.* 4(4).

Muirhead, B. (2001), 'Practical strategies for teaching computer-mediated classes', *Educational technology and society.* 4(2): 1-12.
Muirhead, B. (1999), *Attitudes toward interactivity in a graduate distance education program: A qualitative analysis.* Parkland, Fl: Dissertation.com.

Nichols, M. (2002), *Teaching for Learning.* New Zealand: Traininc.co.nz.

Passerini, K. and Granger, M.J. (2000), 'A developmental model for distance learning using the Internet', *Computers and education*. 34(1): 1-15.

Pokay, P., Langer, G., Boody, R., Petch-Hogan, B. and Rainey, J. (2001), *Exploring a way for teacher candidates to demonstrate student learning* Paper presented at the 81st Annual Conference of Teacher Education, Feb. 17-21, 2001, New Orleans, Louisiana.

Spitzer, D.R. (2001), 'Don't forget the high-touch with the high-tech in distance learning', *Educational technology*. 5(2): 51-55.

Swenson, C. (2001), *New models for higher education: Creating an adult-centered institution*. http://www.ulaval.ca/BI/Globalisation-Universities/pages/actes/Craig-Swenson.pdf (accessed 7April 2003).

University of Phoenix, (2003a), *Fact Book 2003*. University of Phoenix.

University of Phoenix, (2003b), *University of Phoenix Fact Sheet*. University of Phoenix. http://www.phoenix.edu/Factsheet.pdf (accessed 7 April 2003).

Part II

**Into the Unknown: Charting the Future of Virtual
Learning Environments in Higher Education**

Working and Learning Together: ICT-Supported Learning in Small Businesses

Craig Thomson

Abstract

Information and communications technologies (ICT) are central to the lifelong learning policy in the UK. Considerable public expenditure continues to be applied to the creation of on-line learning and on-line learner information services. These are seen as having a major role in stimulating learning in the small business sector which has traditionally proved reluctant to engage in structured programmes of employee development. While policy has resulted in significant spending on new infrastructure, insufficient attention is being paid to the ways in which those in the workplace learn and learn about learning.

The effective development of learning in small businesses is dependent on the radical changes associated with ICT being matched by equally radical changes in the way that work-based learning is conceptualised and organised. This chapter suggests that the development of ICT-supported work-based learning will result in significant changes in learning relationships and in the sources from which learners seek support. In particular, this chapter explores the potential for new learning relationships to be recognised and taken fully into account in planning and implementing work-based learning programmes. While positive for learners and the businesses in which they work, the changes in roles and relationships which the adoption of this perspective will involve will challenge and potentially marginalise traditional players in the learning market.

1. Introduction

This chapter considers a range of points that are of particular relevance in gaining a clearer understanding of information and communications technology (ICT) supported work-based learning and e-learning in small businesses. The context within which this chapter has been prepared is provided by current developments in the UK generally and in Scotland specifically. Following the election of a Labour Government for the UK in 1997, learning rapidly became a central policy theme. This has been re-emphasised by the Scottish Parliament. Since its re-establishment in 1999 (after a gap stretching back to 1707) the Scottish Parliament has taken a vigorous approach to policy and, in line with wider policy objectives in the UK, has placed a high priority on education and training and the use of new technologies. It has described its objectives in these areas as the creation of a "learning nation" and ensuring that Scotland enjoys "... the fullest possible participation in the digital technologies in timescales that bring competitive advantage" (Scottish Executive, 2000; Scottish Executive, 2001). A major inquiry into lifelong learning carried out by the Enterprise and Lifelong Learning Committee of the Parliament and a subsequent strategy statement have confirmed their policy priorities (Scottish Parliament, 2002; Scottish Executive, 2003).

As a consequence of these developments, the last two years of the 1990s and the first three of the new millennium have seen the rapid development of the infrastructure required to enable learning and the provision of information for learners using web-based systems.

The core objectives of lifelong learning policy include stimulating the development and growth of learning in small businesses. A central theme of this chapter is that for this to be achieved it has to be recognised that recent radical developments in learning technology must now be matched by equally radical changes in the ways in which work-based learning in small businesses is understood, organised and supported.

In the following section the term *small business* is briefly defined and explored. This chapter moves on to describe and reflect on direct research with small businesses. Two specific sets of issues are identified and explored as being particularly relevant to understanding and developing work-based learning in small businesses. These relate, firstly, to potential *sources* of learner support in the workplace and, secondly, to the *forms* of support required by learners. As part of this central section of this chapter, the meaning of the term 'work-based learning' is considered and the question of how learners 'learn about learning' in the workplace is addressed briefly. This is followed by a concluding section that reflects on a number of the main points raised.

2.   Small Businesses

Businesses which are either small or are small/medium (SMEs) make up a very significant sector of the economy of the UK (Matlay, 1997, 577). In all but one sector (the exception was the electricity, gas and water supply sector) in 1996 over 99% of all businesses in the UK were SMEs (Hughes and Gray, 1998, 7). This translated into 42% of total national turnover and 46% of non-government employment. This is a pattern which repeats around the world. Internationally, "SMEs - defined broadly as firms with up to 500 employees - typically account for up to 99 per cent of all firms, 60 per cent of employment and 40 - 60 per cent of output in national economies" (UNCTAD, 1998, 1). The broad definition of an SME as a company of up to 500 employees used within this quote is consistent with one of the definitions used by the EU (although EU definitions vary and can also employ a limit of either 250 or 300 employees). Other definitions of 'SME' include those based on criteria relating to growth rate, level of reserves and supply chain issues (Hughes and Gray, 1998, 10).

For the purpose of this chapter, *small business* is used as a term to describe businesses towards the smaller end of the spectrum. Such businesses would typically not, for example, employ specialist human resource managers, operate a training department or enjoy other similar specialist staffing characteristics of larger businesses. Key characteristics of small businesses are:

- the total number of employees is below 100
- the majority of the operation is in one locality (though not necessarily on one site)
- ownership and control remain within the business.

At the other end of the scale, 'small' is not taken to include 'micro', a term that refers to businesses with five or less employees.

While these characteristics relating to size can be used to define small businesses in general terms, attempts to move the definition onto a more specific level tend to be unproductive. Small businesses vary widely in their area of activity and in the ways in which they are organised and operated. The sector includes everything from digital businesses working internationally to local trades (plumbers, electricians, joiners, etc), professions (lawyers, accountants, doctors, etc) and retail businesses. The small business 'sector' encompasses sole traders, partnerships, limited companies, charities and cooperatives.

The scale of the challenge of stimulating learning in small businesses is underlined by the extent to which colleges, universities and other bodies supporting learning have failed to engage successfully with this broad and diverse sector in the past. Working with small businesses can prove difficult, costly and disappointing for organisations involved in education and training (Hughes and Gray, 1998, 10). The smaller the business, the less likely they are to embrace or, more critically, to resource, formal programmes of education and training. As Gibb has pointed out in considering small firms' training and competitiveness, ".... training does not appeal to the small firms population for a variety of obvious reasons relating to time and resource" (Gibb, 1995, 14). Furthermore, low levels of participation in learning in small businesses result only in part from demand-side problems. They can also be attributed to supply side failure in that many of the education and training opportunities that are made available to small businesses are inappropriate in terms of time, cost and location. Matlay draws attention to the point that many of the solutions offered to this sector were developed for other situations and with larger enterprises in mind:

"Expedient attempts to down-scale and forcibly fit large-
scale training strategies to resource-starved small
businesses have resulted in a relative paucity of materials
focusing specifically upon the human resource needs of
smaller firms" (Matlay, 1997, 578).

The shift required to ensure that learning materials and
methodologies are appropriate to small businesses is a significant one and
the assumption that learning relationships (between learners and between
learning providers and learners) that have failed in the past can be dusted
off and used effectively in e-learning has to be recognised as
fundamentally flawed. Indeed, despite the fact that the strong proposition
behind this chapter is that ICT presents exciting and challenging
opportunities, its adoption in work-based situations may eventually prove
to owe as much to the limitations of traditional learning as to the benefits
that new technologies present (Helm, 1997, 41).

3.   Listening to Learners and Developing Models

We now turn to focus on learners in these complex, diverse and
challenging situations by drawing on two simple models. The models serve
two purposes. On the one hand, they can be used as conceptual
methodological devices to 'organise' and to reflect and, on the other, as
practical 'tools' to describe, compare and consider learning situations on
which research focusses. This was based on the position that models offer
"... a form of explanation and are therefore closely related to
understanding" (Lacey, 1993, 127).

The first model illustrates *sources* of support for learners and the
second the *forms* of support. The initial understanding developed and
invested in these models has been used as a basis on which to consider
direct information provided by interviews and other forms of investigation
carried out over the past four years (Thomson, 1999; Pinder and Thomson,
2003). These highlight the wide range of factors that shape the experience
of individual learners in small businesses including: social, learning and
employment backgrounds; roles as employees; learning strategies and
skills; and the extent to which learners found that ICT itself acted as a
gateway or a barrier to learning (mainly a function of their familiarity with
or fear of computers). In addition to these individual characteristics, a
range of broader factors shape the experience of learners in small
businesses including the forms of learning support available, the ability of
learners to interact or engage with this support and, as part of this, by the
social and organisational contexts within which learning takes place and
support for learning is provided. The quality and coherence of learner

opportunity can also be influenced by the lack of specialist human resource management and development skills and capacity in the business.

4.   Learning in the Workplace

The points above relating to collaboration in learning and support for learners in the workplace focus attention on a specific question. What exactly is meant by work-based learning? In addressing this, it is important to bear in mind the primary function of the locations in which it takes place. Pillay et al point out that while workplaces can offer excellent learning opportunities, they are complex learning situations that have other priorities that "...may hinder the learning process" (Pillay et al, 1998, 240). Work-based learning takes place in locations that those involved recognise primarily as workplaces, not learning places. Problems resulting from lack of time, space or priority being applied to learning are common.

Within these complex contexts, the relationship between learning and work can take a number of forms as individuals observe, explore or self-instruct, receive on-the-job instruction, withdraw from the job to learn or are involved in various combinations of these and other options. In attempting to explore and understand this diverse set of potential forms of work-based learning, a useful distinction can be drawn between learning *at* work and learning *for* or *through* work (Reeve et al, 1998, 19).

The work of Jean Lave also presents terms and concepts that are helpful. Lave explores how people work and learn in dynamic, changing and developing contexts in which learning results from direct participation (Lave, 1993). In Lave's view the individual learner does not gain a discrete body of abstract knowledge to transport and reapply in later contexts. Instead, knowledge is acquired by engaging in a range of processes under the attenuated conditions of *legitimate peripheral participation* (Hanks, 1991, 14). Lave emphasises the circularity of the relationship between learning and the workplace in a direct experiential sense; learning takes place in context, results from participation and develops through experience.

Learning in small businesses varies in relation to Lave's concepts between that which is contextualised and that which, in an immediate, concrete or experiential sense, is partly decontextualised. Learners engage in a range of activity including 'fully situated' learning (both supported by and not supported by ICT) in which they were learning through participation as part, for example, of their day-to-day work. It can also include learning by way of transfer (or intentional instruction as Lave would have it) involving the computer as a medium of self-instruction or supported instruction. A further set of activity that emerged from interviews with learners (a point to which I return towards the end of this chapter) involves learning about learning (Thomson, 1999). This can also be viewed as fully situated as learners undertake a form of apprenticeship in learning and develop learning skills and strategies influenced by the culture and behaviour around them in the workplace.

5.   Sources and Forms of Learner Support

In considering ICT-supported learning, it is important to avoid excessive focus on the technology and to emphasise the centrality of learning and the learner. However it is an oversimplification to suggest that technical issues should simply be set aside to allow pedagogy to be given its rightful place. The critical importance of the technology and, related to this, of the nature and format of materials in ICT-supported learning has to be acknowledged and a balance achieved reflecting the fact that '... pedagogy and technology are ... fundamental and inseparable' (Evans and Nation, 1993, 197). This balance is reflected in the first of the models, Model A, which highlights two broad sets of learner interfaces. The first of these, described as *transactional links*, relates to the range of potential supportive inter-personal transactions in which learners in small businesses might engage locally and at a distance. The second interface relates to the technology and the materials delivered or supported by this. These are described as *instrumental connections*.

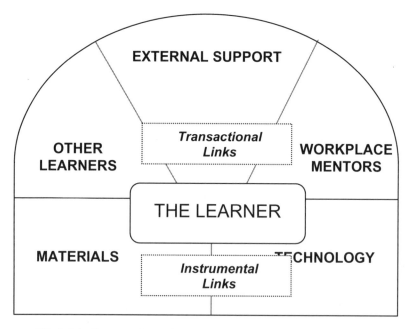

Model A: Learner Interfaces

Model A is based on a third generation view of distance learning (Garrison, 1985; Nipper, 1989; Evans and Nation, 1993; Thorpe, 1998). The key elements of third generation distance learning are interactivity and the integration of new technologies and materials with support for learning (Thorpe, 1998, 270). As such, its development has been tied closely to the emergence of the information society. Garrison describes a "... post-industrial model of teaching and learning at a distance" which "... incorporates highly interactive communications technology along with the ideal of both personalised and collaborative learning" (Garrison, 1997, 3).

The framework within which learners in small businesses collaborate is reflected by the three principal transactional links identified in Model A. These are learners' potential points of contact with external support (such as college or university tutors), in-company support (workplace mentors) and other learners. The transactional links combine with the two principal instrumental connections or 'non-human' points of contact for learners (with learning materials and technology). These various components shape Model A as illustrated.

Model A is not intended to suggest that one simple model (that is, that teachers support learners) can be replaced by another (learners support each other). Rather, it highlights that for the ICT supported learner in the small business of the 21st Century, the range of links used and the emphasis placed on them are likely to vary from learner to learner with the permutations broadly defined by the model. A factor relevant to the successful development of ICT-supported work-based learning that can be drawn from this is that a range of potential forms of support should be available and learners should be clear about how to engage with each potential link in a pattern that meets their specific individual needs. Learning opportunities should be made available in a way that allows "... individualised, cooperative and collaborative kinds of learning to be combined" (Friedrich, 1997, 34).

ICT opens the door to work-based learning in a small business developing as a socially located exercise that rejects ICT supported learning as an individual exercise supported by a single umbilical link to a distant tutor. Much and potentially most of the social interaction can be local (that is, within the business) rather than distant. The lack of specialist or dedicated staff organising, delivering or supporting learning in small businesses makes the potential role of ICT doubly important in this respect.

While Model A identifies a set of points of interaction for learners, it does not include any indication of the forms of support required or provided at each interface. Rather than attempting to integrate these in (and complicating) the same model, these points are incorporated in a separate, linked model (Model B). The development of this followed a similar pattern to Model A. However, the initial outline drew significantly on a single source. In the mid-1980s during a period in which increasing priority was being placed in the UK on open learning as the way forward in further education, the Manpower Services Commission (MSC) funded the National Extension College to produce an 'Open Learning Toolkit'. Extracts from this include the identification of the key roles of managers/teachers in open learning schemes when supporting learners (Lewis and Spencer, 1986, 94). Their work has largely managed to stand the test of time in that it has provided a basis on which to model the principal forms of learner support relevant to work-based learners in the 21st Century.

As with Model A the development of Model B drew on interaction and interviews carried out with learners. A major distinction between the two models is that while ICT-supported learning creates new sources of support, different points of contact and new collaborative relationships for learners in small businesses, it can be argued that the *scope* of support required by these learners does not differ significantly from that required by them in traditional (same time/same place) settings.

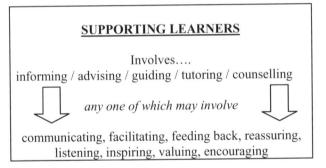

Model B: Learner Support

Although the shape of Model B was influenced by the MSC Toolkit and its subsequent use by Lewis and Spencer, the assumptions behind it differ significantly. The assumption that the principal (or, indeed, the sole) relationship relevant to the learner is that with her tutor or teacher is rejected. Models A and B reflect the view that college, university or other tutors are simply one of a range of possible sources of help and support available to the learner. Internal support in the workplace is viewed as a central factor in this form of work-based learning.

The individual points relating to learner behaviour and expectations that shaped Models A and B are set within a complex context. Various internal priorities in small businesses combine with systems, structure and other factors to complicate or simplify, reward or discourage and displace or accommodate learning. Small businesses each have their own cultures, relationships, rules and objectives. These shape how people work together and set the context within which they can learn together. Similarly, learners present distinct pictures of themselves as learners, workers and individuals. The organisational and cultural context of businesses are critical in shaping work-based learning and in setting internal limits to variation in the learning context. These limits are both implicit in terms of norms of behaviour (including learning behaviour and expectations) and explicit where tasks and standards of performance are specified in the form of job descriptions and learning plans (Scribner, 1984, 15).

Within the complex working and learning context of the small business, individuals develop their own assumptions about and commitment to learning and their learning skills and strategies. This can be viewed as a form of apprenticeship model consistent with views of apprenticeship and communities of practice set out by Fuller and Unwin who point out that such communities in the workplace are:

> "... not only defined geographically, but also by the connections and relationships that are developed between its members and between them and the activity that brings them together" (Fuller and Unwin, 1998, 158).

New learners in such situations begin to learn and, closely influenced by their colleagues, to learn about learning. Their understanding and expectations about learning in the workplace (that is, in the specific workplace in which they are located) are critically influenced by the behaviour and expectations of their co-participants. Small businesses conform to the characteristics of communities of practice set out by Wenger (Wenger, 1998). Where behaviour is positive and expectations are high, this can be expected to influence new employees and new learners in the workplace positively as they work out the meaning of learning in that location. Within the workplace (as in other situations) "... people in activity are skilful at, and are more often than not engaged in, helping each other to participate in changing ways in a changing world" (Lave, 1993, 5).

6. Concluding Points

ICT has the potential to stimulate the construction of new models and relationships in which access to and take up of learning in small businesses can be increased within structured programmes of relevant, appropriate education and training. Recent progress with the development of technology, environments and materials has been impressive. However, it cannot simply be assumed that better learning results from more technology, more challenging instructional media and more interactivity by way of communications media (Thorpe 1998, 271). Furthermore, little will be achieved if ICT is simply used as a medium to rework inflexible forms of interaction with small businesses and work-based learners that have failed in the past or to repackage learning solutions developed for larger work-based situations. Four sets of points are highlighted in this conclusion.

Firstly, work-based learning has to be recognised as multi-dimensional. It takes place in a variety of formal and informal situations, is based on a wide range of activities and encompasses a broad spectrum from hands-on activity to abstract learning. The format in which opportunities are presented and organised for learners has to be sufficiently flexible to reflect this diversity and to do so in a way that recognises that learning tends to be viewed as a secondary, optional activity in the workplace.

Secondly, and building on this point, learning environments and materials and the provision of support for learners have to be developed in a way that encourages and accommodates both the intricate patterns of collaboration and co-participation that exist between learners and the complex interaction between learners and the workplace as a learning site. ICT creates the opportunity to develop new relationships based on new technologies and new materials. Ever-faster telecommunications should be harnessed to support the development of mutually supportive communities of learners composed of interdependent individuals. This will require the further development of learning support methodologies that recognise and foster both personalised and collaborative approaches to learning.

Thirdly, the lack of specialist human resource management capacity in small businesses has to be recognised as an important factor. Small businesses are most likely to engage with learning when its organisation and management are uncomplicated and when learning tasks and content can be related directly to business need and business development. It is important that technology, environments, materials and methodology all combine to support the management of learning and the development of explicit links between learning and the needs of the business.

Finally, the successful stimulation of learning in small businesses is critically dependent on the development of a new understanding of the sources of support that learners require and a clear appreciation of the forms of support most appropriate to them. As collaborative learning between and among learners develops, contact with colleagues and other learners and the availability of more comprehensive, self-contained and inspiring learning materials are likely to mean that learners can increasingly be expected to view traditional forms of tutor support as optional, distant features. Changes associated with the information society, with the emergence of third generation distance learning and with the history and inherent characteristics of work-based learning in small businesses are fundamentally changing the 'geography' of learning. These changes are resulting in a move from distance *learning* to distance *tutoring*. ICT shifts the organisation, support and assessment of learning more firmly into a freestanding format in the workplace and, as a result, represents a challenge to the distance and traditional learning establishments to re-conceptualise radically their relationships with the small business sector.

In the absence of an understanding of and a willingness to address points such as these, current broad policies in the UK aimed at the development of a learning society and specific lifelong learning initiatives such as SUfI will fail to attract and to benefit individual learners and workers and the small businesses in which they are employed.

References

Evans, T. and Nation, D. (1993), *Reforming open and distance education.* London: Kogan Page.

Friedrich, F. (1997), 'Transfer of learning technologies – the experience of the DELTA DEMO ESC Project', *Open Learning,* 13(2): 51-57.

Fuller, A and Unwin, L. (1998), 'Reconceptualising apprenticeship: exploring the relationships between work and learning', *Journal of Vocational Education and Training,* 50(2): 153-171.

Garrison, D. (1985), 'Three generations of technological innovation in distance education', *Distance Education,* 6(2): 235-241.

Garrison, D. (1997), 'Computer conferencing: the post industrial age of distance education', *Journal of Open and Distance Education,* 12(2): 3-11.

Gibb, A. (1995), 'Small firms' training and competitiveness: building upon the small business as a learning organisation', *International Small Business Journal,* 15:(3) 13-29.

Hanks, W. (1991), Foreword in: Lave, J. and Wenger, E. (eds.) *Situated learning: Legitimate peripheral participation.* Cambridge: Cambridge University Press.

Helm, P. (1997), 'Teaching and learning with the new technologies: for richer, for poorer, for better, for worse', in: Field, J. (ed.) *Electronic Pathways*, Leicester: NIACE.

Hughes, M. and Gray, S. (1998), *Promoting learning in small and medium sized enterprises*. Coventry: The Further Education Funding Council.

Lacey, C. (1993), 'Problems of sociological fieldwork: a review of the methodology of Hightown Grammar', in: Hammersley, M. (ed.) *Educational Research: Current Issues*. London: Open University Press.

Lave, J (1993), 'The practice of learning', in: Chaiklin, S. and Lave, J. (eds.) *Understanding practice: perspectives on activity and context*. Cambridge, Cambridge University Press.

Lewis, R. and Spencer, D. (1986), *What is open learning?* Cambridge: Cambridge University Press.

Nipper, S. (1989), 'Third generation distance learning and computer conferencing', in Mason, R. and Kaye, A. (eds.) *Mindweave: communication, computers and distance education*. Oxford: Pergammon.

Matlay, H. (1997), 'The paradox of training in the small business sector of the British economy', *Journal of Vocational Education and Training* 49(4): 573-589.

Pillay, H., Brownlee, J. and McCrindle, A. (1998), 'The influence of individuals' beliefs about learning and nature of knowledge on educating a competent workforce', *Journal of education and work* 11(3), 239-254.

Pinder, S. and Thomson, C. (2003), 'Small business: big challenge', *Conference proceedings: Fourth International Conference on Human System Learning*. Glasgow: Glasgow Caledonian University.

Reeve, F., Gallacher, J. and Mayes, T. (1998), 'Can new technology remove barriers to learning?', *Open learning* 13(3), 18-26.

Scottish Executive (2000), *Scotland: the learning nation*. Edinburgh: Scottish Executive Publications.

Scottish Executive (2001), *Digital inclusion: Connecting Scotland's people*. Edinburgh: Scottish Executive Publications.

Scottish Executive (2003), *Learning thorugh life: Life through learning.* Edinburgh: Scottish Executive Publications.

Scottish Parliament Enterprise and Lifelong Learning Committee (2002), *Inquiry into lifelong learning, final report.* Edinburgh: Scottish Parliament.

Scribner, S. (1984), 'Studying Working Intelligence', in: Rogoff, B. and Lave, J. (eds.) *Everyday cognition: its development in social context.* Cambridge, Mass.: Harvard University Press.

Thomson, C. (1999), *Developing information and communications technology supported work-based learning in small and medium sized enterprises:* Thesis submitted for the degree of Doctor of Education. University of Sheffield.

Thomson, C. (2003), 'Further education', in: Bryce, T. and Humes, W. *Scottish Education (2nd Edition).* Edinburgh: Edinburgh University Press.

Thorpe, M. (1998), 'Assessment and third generation distance education', *Distance Education,* 19(2): 265-286.

UNCTAD (1998), *Note to correspondents No 44,* http:/www.unctad.org/em/pub/pu98guen.htm

Wenger, E. (1998), *Communities of practice: Learning, meaning and identity.* Cambridge: Cambridge University Press.

Strategic and Pedagogic Requirements for Virtual Learning in the Context of Widening Participation

Mark Stiles

Abstract

The necessity for institutional strategies to overtly address the professional development of staff is discussed in the dual contexts of the educational needs of widening participation and inclusion and the pedagogic challenges these bring. In particular, it is posited that traditional models of teaching and learning as practised in higher education may well be inadequate for the "new" higher education and the need for the adoption of active pedagogies which may well be unfamiliar to, or at least unpractised by, many academic staff is considered.

Alongside these issues, the pressures on both higher education (HE) and further education (FE) sectors to adopt the use of Managed and Virtual Learning Environments are counterpoised. The author argues that these pressures, which are political, economic and commercial, are leading to a process of selection and adoption of systems which seriously underestimates the pedagogic challenges and which may lead to the business and educational processes of institutions becoming constrained by their adopted technologies.

It is concluded that, given the evidence of earlier failures in learning technology to produce sustainable impact on practice, the cumulative effect of the problems and pressures discussed may lead to the current round of adoption of e-learning systems becoming shorter-lived than expected by those involved.

1. Widening Participation and Social Inclusion

The current profile of learners in UK higher education is not that of the small elite of 20 or 30 years ago. Even the "Age Participation Index" - the DfES measure of the number of young (under 21) home initial entrants expressed as a percentage of the averaged 18- to 19-year-old population - which rose gradually from 6% in 1961 to 19% in 1990 had increased to 34% by 1998 (DfES, 2001). However, modern HE learners are drawn from a much wider spectrum than before. There is a very high proportion of non-traditional students from a wide range of social backgrounds including single parents and returners to education - those seeking professional updating and other forms of lifelong learning. By 1997 this pattern of change was already well documented (Dearing, 1997, 7.1-7.16). The continuing drive into widening participation and lifelong learning, with a government agenda aiming at 50% participation in HE within the 18-30 age group and other targets relating to participation by adults, means that the impact of this change on the overall learner profile can only increase (DfES, 2001). Areas of low participation now being addressed include those related to social inclusion with participation from social class V being seen as an important target (National Audit Office, 2002a, 8). It is worth noting here however that ministers admit that the goal of increased numbers could be reached without meeting those goals aimed at inclusion (Thomson, 2002). With the increased provision of HE within FE institutions, including the introduction of Foundation Degrees, the profile of the HE learner becomes even more diverse.

2.   Factors Affecting 'Widening Participation' Learners

Diversity, coupled with the financial expediencies of being a modern student, means that the motivation and needs of 'widening participation' learners are different from the traditional post-A-level HE student. A recent survey noted that whilst employment and career aspirations had become prime motivators for all learners entering HE, for non-traditional students this factor was further amplified (Clark et al, 2002, 12). Mature entrants incorporated these aspirations into an overall desire to achieve a "change of life" and were highly motivated at the point of entering HE. Needs among 'widening participation' groups entering higher education include location and childcare facilities and, particularly, for those learning part-time or in-work, the timing of course activities to suit these constraints (Clark et al, 2002, 14) (Young and Morris, 2000, 19-20).

Even once non-traditional learners are in higher education, their needs are still important. For example, reasons for non-completion by students include:

- Lack of preparedness for higher education
- Changing personal circumstances or interests
- Financial matters
- Impact of undertaking paid work
- Dissatisfaction with the course or institution

(National Audit Office, 2002b, 11).

In terms of meeting goals relating to social inclusion, it is worth noting that working class students perceive debt more negatively than those from other social classes – this acts as a barrier to recruitment and retention and must increase the negative impact of undertaking paid work (Woodrow and Yorke, 2002, 168).

Interestingly, most of the UK government reports thus far referenced do not cite the ability to learn flexibly as a major factor influencing entrance to higher education among those in targeted 'widening participation' or inclusion groups. The question must be asked whether, given the reasons for non-completion quoted above, would retention not be enhanced by institutions not only being able to accommodate flexible learning and attendance patterns but also by being able to respond more flexibly to learners changing needs? This is an issue affecting inclusion and accessibility and is regarded as good practice in both (Doyle and Robson, 2002).

3. The Impact on 'Widening Participation' Learners

Financial pressures on students attending to a traditional pattern, which are frequently addressed by students undertaking paid employment, are paralleled by time pressures on students learning in-work or part-time. These, and other pressures such as child-care issues and studying with disabilities, all have one common impact: learners have increasingly constrained time to undertake study. This means that the workload imposed on learners is effectively increased. Additional pressure is applied to 'widening participation' learners by over-assessment - the impact of assessment load on both students and staff is a recurring theme in institutional learning and teaching strategies (LTSN Generic Centre, 2002, 17).

It is recognized that learners will adopt different approaches to learning according to their personal preferences and the context in which they are learning and that the two are interdependent (Entwistle, 1987). Excessive workload is one factor associated with the adoption by learners of a "surface" approach to learning (Chambers, 1992; Entwistle and Tait 1990). Given the additional pressures on 'widening participation' and inclusion learners, the author would posit that it is likely, even where curriculum and pedagogy are attuned to the desire to promote a deep approach, such learners are likely to be driven by expediency towards the adoption of 'achieving' or strategic approaches as a means of coping with their studies (Entwistle, 1997).

Taking into account the strong emphasis, noted earlier, on career aspirations and employment within these groups of learners and the important fact that many of the major pressures on them are outside the control of course designers and tutors, it may be necessary to recognize that a high proportion of learners will in the future be strategic in their approach and for institutions to take this into account in the design of learning experiences.

4. The Challenge to Curriculum and Pedagogy

Fundamental to the following discussion is the proposition that the design of the learning experience and the content of the course are mutually interdependent; decisions concerning how students will learn (form) and what they will learn (content) are interconnected. In 1997 Dearing noted:

"Planning for learning means that designing the forms of
instruction which support learning becomes as important
as preparing the content of programmes" (Dearing, 1997,
8.13).

There is a need for institutions to address within their curriculum
the developmental needs of non-traditional learners and most institutions
have taken steps in this direction. Provision for this can be separate where
provision is specifically targeted at non-traditional learners or integrated
where provision is aimed at developing requisite capabilities in all learners
(Warren, 2002). Warren argues strongly for the integrated approach as the
best means of meeting both the widening participation and skills agendas.

This view is in concurrence with that of this author who has
previously argued that the development of the use of meaning-making or
semiotic tools which are specific to given disciplines or professions and the
reapplication of the tools and practices of the given culture, coupled with
recognition of the relatedness of tacit and codified knowledge in the
context of tasks or problems, is fundamental to the development of
expertise (Stiles 2000a). This supports a view that skills are more likely to
be transferable when developed in an authentic context, rather than treated
in a separate, generic way.

The need to encompass the diversity of all learners and the
different experiences they bring to the learning context requires that a
greater understanding of appropriate pedagogic practices is required of
staff. Practices that are effective for the non-traditional student are likely to
be effective for all learners (Woodrow and York, 2002, 169). The author
suggests that this implies an increasing move to, or at least a wider
understanding of, constructivist approaches encompassing theories on the
social nature of learning situated learning and cognitive apprenticeship and
models of learning such as the conversational model (Vygotsky, 1978;
Brown et al, 1989; Lave, 1988; Laurillard, 1993).

Learning activities and assessment need to be authentic - normal
to the culture in question and involving its tools and artefacts - and to
address the needs of the skills and lifelong learning agendas (Brown et al,
1989; Kearsley and Shneiderman, 1998; Elton and Johnston, 2002, ch 3).
Both learning activity and assessment need to reward understanding and be
clearly related to syllabus (Entwistle, 1987). Entwistle also notes that the
learner's current level of development must be matched in terms of
assessment, content and resources. For 'widening participation' students
this has implications for the *size* of curricula. Chambers noted:

"...teachers may actually need to restrict the scope of a
curriculum, especially in the early stages of students'

careers, in order to make the time and provide incentives for them to behave appropriately" (Chambers, 1992, 145).

The issue of curriculum scope impinges on another area, that of fostering creativity and problem-solving abilities in undergraduate courses. A report commissioned by the UK LTSN Generic Centre noted that such fostering requires space at time a time when resources, student diversity and time pressures are major constraints to innovation of curricula (McGoldrick, 2002). The same report notes the lack of preparedness for higher education in many students described earlier.

5.   The UK HE Context
The expansion of participation has taken place without much reference to how people learn and the quality of the learning experience provided (Pring, 2001). Where institutions are committed to widening participation the cost of supporting the 'widening participation' learners greatly exceeds additional available funding to support them, and 'subsidy' is provided by (unpaid) staff time (Boxall et al, 2002). In 1997, Dearing commented:

> "Our survey and other research suggest that lectures are still the most common form of teaching in higher education. Initial findings from research suggest that many staff still see teaching primarily in terms of transmission of information, mainly through lectures" (Dearing, 1997, 8.14).

Although much progress has since been made in widening the range of delivery, it is still the case that the lecture remains the majority tool. In the context of widening participation it is worth noting Bligh's view that lectures are not the best way to promote thought, are relatively ineffective at teaching skills and should not usually be used to change learners' attitudes (Bligh, 1988). Lectures can be viewed as content-driven, context-driven or pedagogy-driven with students responding more favourably to the more pedagogically-driven lecture (Saroyan and Snell, 1997).
        Assessment is also an issue with innovation still relatively uncommon (Race, 2001). A recent critical review of assessment commented "...even the best of current practices are by and large not good practice" (Elton and Johnston, 2002, 4.1).
        This is a worrying state of affairs given recognition of the need for diversity in assessment methods to enhance the effectiveness of

learning and teaching, particularly (but not solely) in the context of widening participation and inclusion. It is both ironic and significant that this need is commonly recognised in institutional strategies but clearly not as widely practiced (LTSN Generic Centre, 2002).

Other problems are more practical; students regularly complain of the lack of availability of teaching staff and of problems with the quality, consistency, and timeliness of feedback (National Audit Office, 2002b). Failure to recognise the central importance of pedagogy also extends to those involved in supporting learning. For example, the INSPIRAL report commented "[Pedagogic] issues have a history of being ignored by librarians in particular" (Currier, 2001, 5.2.3.2).

An LTSN report notes the place of the "hidden curriculum", where certain learning was implicit rather than explicit and depended on sources such as attitude and behaviour of peers and academics (McGoldrick, 2002). This report also notes the importance of students drawing on ideas beyond the subject curriculum as a vital component of creativity and effective problem solving. The issue of synthesis as a vital component of fostering creativity has raised an interesting question and challenge. A recent paper notes that of all of the components of Blooms taxonomy, synthesis is the most resistant to assessment via technology and raises the question "is synthesis actually the highest order of learning competence?" (Fuller, 2002).

6.   The Potential of Technology

The Dearing Report was very positive about the potential of Communications and Information Technologies "C&IT" to enhance the "quality, flexibility and effectiveness of higher education" and to provide "improved access and increased effectiveness, particularly in terms of lifelong learning". Since that time, there has been an explosion in the adoption of systems such as Virtual Learning Environments and national organisations such as the Joint Information Systems Committee (JISC) have funded numerous initiatives and projects in the area of the use of technology to support the teaching and learning process and its management (Jenkins et al, 2001).

The author agrees that the potential is there for the creation of learning environments that will meet the needs of the modern, diverse learner and widen access to higher education still further (Stiles, 2002). Importantly, they may give teaching staff more opportunity to actually communicate with students (JM Consulting, 2002, 26). However, this enthusiasm is not based on a history that evidences much large-scale success in terms of effectiveness. The author has previously described reasons for failure in the use of technology in learning as being based on:

- Failure to engage the learner
- Mistaking "interactivity" for engagement
- Focusing on content rather than outcomes
- Mirroring traditional approaches on the technology
- Failure to recognise the social nature of learning
- Seeing discourse as the prime collaborative form

(Stiles, 2000b).

This is not a unique view; surveys have found staff think first in terms of delivery approaches and converting traditional courses into electronic forms is common (Tomes and Higgison, 1998, 25; Phillips, 1998). In the use of Virtual Learning Environments (VLE) in most institutions there is a clear focus on the conversion of traditional lecture programmes, emphasising the distribution of materials followed by assignments and tests with pedagogy remaining based largely on the traditional (Maher et al, 2001; Birchall et al, 2002; Littlejohn 2002). A recent HEFCE Issues paper noted: "Currently PowerPoint slides are hung off the universities' Managed Learning Environments (MLE) whereas their role should be much greater" (JM Consulting, 2002, 32).

Those working in learning development and learning technology are almost unanimous in emphasising the need for adoption of active, learner-centred learning paradigms based on constructivist principles including the need for peer interaction and collaboration (Beaty et al, 2002, Martin, 2001), (Ramsey 2002). The author has emphasised the central position of authentic activity in this context (Stiles 2000b).

7.   The Practice Gap

So why is there a gap between what is perceived by experts as good practice and the mainstream reality? The author proposes a number of interconnected factors: staff development; institutional strategies and pressures; sector wide pressures; technology issues.

These factors will be considered in turn, beginning with staff development. Despite the recommendations of Dearing in 1997 the following comment was made in 2002:

"If networked e-learning is to become a rich and robust educational practice providing quality learning environments, practitioners need to engage in critical and reflexive evaluation of their own practice. Any shift in tutor role as proposed here needs to be supported through professional development. Such professional development should mirror and be consistent with the principles underlying networked e-learning" (Beaty et al, 2002, 6).

The need to provide staff with enhanced opportunities to gain skills and knowledge in pedagogy and learning activity design has been frequently noted in the context of e-learning (Littlejohn 2002; Jenkins et al, 2001; Stiles and Orsmond, 2002). The teaching workforce in HE is still largely untrained and practice is thus unsurprisingly based on what the workforce experienced as a undergraduates themselves. As a result, HE in particular tends to focus on curriculum design rather than on the design of the learning experience itself. Lack of staff development is also a contributory factor in problems with assessment:

> "...until management gives adequate time and resources for all academic teachers to engage in the kind of training and continuing professional development which the latter consider essential for every profession except their own, and academics are then prepared to engage in it, little of significance will change" (Elton and Johnston, 2002, ch 4).

An LTSN study showed that where staff had successfully addressed the pedagogic (and technical) challenges associated with using a VLE, this also had an impact on the pedagogic approaches taken in traditional delivery (Holland and Arrowsmith, 2000).

It is worth considering at this point whether the pedagogic weakness of much e-learning as practiced is not compounded by teaching staff lacking associated technical skills. The iRISSt project noted that staff development officers had low expectations of the technical skills required by teaching staff and that staff with restricted technical skills were as a result likely to restrict the learning opportunities of their students (Garrett et al, 2002).

In short, is the lack of pedagogic development of staff combining with a lack of sophistication in the use of IT to encourage the adoption of bland but technically undemanding approaches? This point is expanded on later.

With regard to institutional strategy, most institutions include the use of e-learning/VLE/MLE in institutional strategy although this is more prevalent in post-1992 Higher Educational Institutions (HEI) (Jenkins et al, 2001). The drivers for adoption are local, regional, national and international. They include issues of:

- Widening access and inclusion

- Employability and skills
- Providing flexibility for full-time students in part-time employment
- Government demands on quality, monitoring etc
- Government policy on working with industry and commerce
- Globalisation of HE and new competitors
- Creation of new partnerships
- Development of new markets and provision

(Smith 2002, Stiles 2000b).

However, recent reports have highlighted the rarity of whole-institution strategies for implementation of VLEs/MLEs. Highlighted in particular are the needs for many institutions to: find approaches to build on existing localised initiatives; address pedagogy; understand the difference between MLEs, which are essentially processes, and VLEs, which are essentially software systems to support learning (Boys, 2002; Condron and Sutherland, 2002). Lack of institutional strategy is also seen as a common barrier to adoption (Smith, 2002).

There are numerous sector-wide barriers to the successful development of e-learning in UK HE/FE and those associated with elements of widening participation and inclusion have already been discussed. Many of the other pressures are economic (reducing unit of resource) and based on central funding activities such as the Research Assessment Exercise (RAE).

Dearing held out the promise of efficiencies from the use of technology in learning. However, analysis of cost-benefits for learning technology was at that that time (and still is) ill-formed (Boucher, 1998). Certainly, the commercial sector see e-learning as a major area of cost saving (Lamb, 2002). In UK HE/FE, the costing of e-learning is much more complex. The implementation and development of VLEs and, particularly, MLEs confronts institutions with a range of challenges which are by their nature very expensive (Boys, 2002; Condron and Sutherland, 2002). One side effect of this has been an understandable national preoccupation with content and its production. Organisations are concerned with the availability of resources, the cost of their production and the problems of content shelf life. On the international stage, problems concerning the national cultural bias of content have been highlighted and there is recognised need for the "chunking" and re-purposing of content (Khakhar, 1999). It is understandable that content and its production is seen as an area where savings are possible but the willingness of staff to share their content is a possible barrier. There are clear contradictions here with many seeing content as a future market and others proposing an opposite model. An unresolved question is: "Is it an institution's content or the educational experience it provides which affects competitive advantage?" Clearly those involved in such initiatives as the Open Knowledge Initiative think the latter is the case (MIT, 2001). There is clear recognition of the complexity of the issues in post-16 education but in the UK the majority of initiatives under the Government e-learning strategy have a strong content or resources bias (Brown, 2002). The author proposes that unless the balance between efforts on content and issues of pedagogy and the support for learning is equalised there is a danger of the current position of the ineffective re-creation of traditional approaches within VLEs being amplified.

For the purposes of this paper, discussion of technology issues will be confined to technological issues surrounding the use of VLEs and MLEs.

The view that VLEs are not pedagogically neutral in their use has been previously proposed by the author and others (Stiles, 2001a; Britain and Liber, 1999; Milligan 1999). It has been noted that VLEs can be prescriptive in their pedagogical approach (Currier, 2001). The author has for some years been associated with the development of a VLE aimed at facilitating active learning paradigms (The COSE Project - www.staffs.ac.uk/COSE). Where issues of induction of learners into the educational rationale have been addressed, and staff have engaged with the pedagogic issues this active learning has proved to be successful and popular with learners (Simpson et al, 2002; Holland and Arrowsmith, 2000). Other systems aimed at active paradigms have also been developed - see for example Colloquia at www.colloquia.net. Mainstream commercial systems are generally characterised as "content-centred" (Milligan 1999). Milligan also proposes that different VLEs suit different learner groups more effectively. Given this pedagogic bias, is it not reasonable to assume that, where staff are taking different pedagogic approaches within an institution, no single VLE system can meet all educational needs?

Returning to the topic of content, the sharing and reuse of content is recognised as an important factor for progress and the development of international specifications such as IMS and SCORM for the packaging and exchange of content are now well advanced. However, the specifications from these organisations relating to maintaining the pedagogic structure and nature of content are much less well advanced. IMS are developing specifications for Simple Sequencing and Learning Design but these are as yet only in public draft form. This is seen as an important issue as, without a way of moving content between systems which preserves its pedagogic intent, content moved from one system to another becomes a series of disaggregated components which requires re-aggregation to become a useful learning opportunity (Perry et al, 2002).

Not all VLE systems have the facility to re-aggregate and re-purpose content once imported, and the pedagogic skills required to do this have already been identified as a problem area. A second problem is that until specifications for Learning Design emerge, available specifications from both IMS and ADL currently focus on individual learning and do not take account of communication and collaboration in learning (Wilson, 2002).

Developments in joining up VLEs with MIS systems, authentication servers, digital libraries and portals and others systems to form MLEs are still very much in their infancy. Recent developments in the UK have tended to focus on enabling institutions to satisfy the demands of funding bodies rather than on the business and educational needs of institutions themselves (Stiles, 2001b). The goal of providing both tutor and learner with a joined-up learning experience that combines effectively traditional and virtual learning and its management with access to local, national and international resources is a worthy one but specifications are not complete and, given that interoperability standards do not provide a plug-and-play solution to interoperability, the creation of MLEs still poses significant challenges and development costs.

The match between systems and institutional strategies is an area of concern. In late 2001, the author carried out a piece of (albeit somewhat imprecise) research on this issue. Members of a number of email discussion lists covering practitioners in e-learning, learning technologists, and other decision influencers such as IT directors were asked the question "If you have an institutional virtual/managed learning environment, what was THE main reason you chose the one you did?"

One hundred and twenty three institutions responded, with some providing responses from more than one individual (often with different responses). It is recognized that institutions must (or, at least, should) have considered a number of factors but the purpose of the survey question was to assess people's perceptions of main priorities. Ten of those who responded (reasonably) insisted on giving more than one reason and only two replies criticised the methodology of the survey. Twenty one people expressed a negative view of their institutions' choice including one IT Director who commented: *"I don't know, I wasn't consulted".*

Reasons for choice were categorized and ranked as follows:

Ease of use in general	31
Ease of use for staff	30
Cost	21
Flexibility/Versatility	16
Integration with MIS	15
Widely used	14
Functionality/Features	13

Pedagogic/Educational Effectiveness/Appropriateness	13
Imposed/A mystery	10
Own system	10
Integration with existing systems/Interoperability	9
Piloted by department/Enthusiasts	6
Neighbour/Partner had it	5
Ease of upload	5
Offline facilities	5
Use more than one	5
Free/Cheap trial	3
Don't want to be left behind	2
Scalability	2
Reliability	2
Value for money	2
Ease of support	2
Ease of use by students	1
Ease of exit	1
Firewall compatibility	1
Salesperson	1

Clearly, this information is open to multiple interpretations. There is however an underlying recognition of the need to get teaching staff involved, probably coupled with institutional concerns not to be left behind by their competitors. Concerns with administrative and organisational issues are also a significant thread. Very few replies evidenced any strong link to particular aspects of organisational strategy. Most of the responses concerning flexibility were of the "not forcing particular approaches to teaching on staff" theme. This might indicate a commendable focus on the quality of the learning experience or, more likely, the author would contend, a reinforcement of the duplication of traditional approaches on the technology discussed earlier. Given the earlier argument that individual VLEs are not pedagogically neutral and that different VLEs may suit different contexts, it is difficult to see how the adoption of a single product can meet the requirements of a positive interpretation of 'flexibility'.

Returning to the comments earlier regarding the effect of a lack of both pedagogic and technical skills on the part of course designers on the way that VLEs are employed, what contribution does an emphasis on "ease of use" as applied to VLE selection have on this? Respondents to the email survey mentioned words such as "intuitive" in the context of VLEs and "complexity of interface" is perceived a negative attribute of products (Simpson et al, 2002). However the view has long been held that "intuitive" in the context of interfaces actually equates to "familiar" and that all interfaces actually have be to learned (Raskin, 1994). So where does this leave us? We have systems being selected by staff whose IT skills are, in reality, modest and whose lack of these skills will also hamper them in seeing the potential of systems for innovating learning. Add to these the lack of innovation in mainstream teaching, learning and assessment and we have a situation where VLE systems are being chosen on the basis of largely being unthreatening with the resulting blandness mentioned earlier.

8.   Conclusion

Institutions, and teaching staff feel pressured to adopt technology-supported learning. The diversity of the learner population is increasing and presenting an ever-wider range of needs and prior experience. Pressures on learners are impacting on their approach to learning and a need for flexibility in provision is emerging. Diversity raises questions of curriculum, pedagogy and assessment, all of which, as practised, remain largely conservative. Despite the increasing potential of technology to support diversity and widened participation, currently its use reflects the same conservatism. Pressures on institutions and staff may be reinforcing this condition rather than acting as agents to change it. Institution strategies are not effectively addressing issues of pedagogy or the introduction of learning technologies. Technological decisions are not being made with a clear focus on what institutions are trying to achieve and staff are not being encouraged or enabled to focus on educational goals before making decisions about the pedagogic approach required and the technology to be used to deliver and support it. Work on specifications for interoperation of technologies is progressing rapidly but are still not yet sufficiently in place to enable the longer term goals of MLEs to be achieved. Standards have been somewhat over-sold and are possibly being exploited by vendors selling to institutions who do not fully understand the true position.

The author proposes that unless there is a national focus on the aspects of e-learning concerned with form (pedagogy and assessment) which is aimed at bringing these into balance with the current focuses on content (curriculum and resources) and issues of technology, students will be increasingly provided with isolating and passive learning experiences which in turn will impact most negatively on those very learners which the government is concerned to involve in FE/HE participation. This negative impact could well disillusion those staff who are currently becoming involved in the use of technology for the first time and may result in a backlash among teaching staff and university managers, resulting in a set-back to the achievement of national goals and competitiveness.

References

Beaty, E., Hodgson, V., Mann, S., and McConnell, D. (2002), *Towards E-Quality in Networked E-Learning in Higher Education*, ESRC [online] , csalt.lancs.ac.uk/esrc/manifesto.htm.

Birchall, D. Smith, M. Schofield, N. Rylance-Watson, E. Burgoyne, J. (2002), *The current and future contribution of e-learning to management and leadership development. Part 1: business schools*, Council for excellence in management and leadership, [online], www.managementandleadershipcouncil.org/reports/r19_1.htm.

Bligh, D. (1998), *What's the Use of Lectures?, 2nd ed.* Exeter: Intellect.
Boucher, A. (1998), 'Information Technology-based teaching and learning in Higher Education: a view of the economic issues', *Journal of information technology for teacher education*, 7(1), 87-111.

Boxall, M., Amin, S., and Baloch, A. (2002), *Determining the Costs of Widening Participation: Report of Pilot Study,* Universities UK and HEFCE, [online], www.universitiesuk.ac.uk/wideningparticipation/

Boys, J. (2002), *Managed Learning Environments, joined* up systems and the problems of organisational change, JISC [online], www.jisc.ac.uk/pub02/mle-organisation.html

Britain, A. and Liber, O. (1999), *A Framework for Pedagogical Evaluation of Virtual Learning,* University of Wales Bangor [online] , www.jtap.ac.uk/reports/htm/jtap-041.html

Brown, J. (2002), *DELG - Outline Draft Report Version 1.1*, Learning and Skills Council DELG 02/018 [online], www.nln.ac.uk/delg/papers/DELG%2002%20018.pdf

Brown, J.S., Collins, A. and Duguid, P. (1989), 'Situated cognition and the culture of learning', *Education research,* 18(1), 32-42.

Chambers, E.A. (1992), 'Workload and the quality of student learning', *Studies in Higher Education*, 17(2), 141-153.

Clark, S., Hill. E., Holmes, J., Palmer, A. and Sharp R. (2002), *Paving the Way.* UCAS.

Condron, F., and Sutherland, S. (2002), *Learning Environments Support in the UK Further and Higher Education Communities*, JISC [online], Available as: www.jisc.ac.uk/pub02/learn_env_sppt_intro.html

Currier, S. (2001), *INPIRAL – InveStigating Portals for Information Resources And Learning – Final Report*. Glasgow: University of Strathclyde.   Available   as: inspiral.cdlr.strath.ac.uk/documents/INSPfinrep.pdf.

Dearing, R. (1997), *Higher Education in the Learning Society*. HMSO.

DfES (2001), *Education and Skills: Delivering Results - A Strategy to 2006*. DfES Publications.

Doyle, C. and Robson, K. (2002), *Accessible curricula - good practice for all*. Cardiff: UWIC Press.

Elton, L. and Johnston, B. (2002), *Assessment in Universities: a critical review of research*, York, LTSN [online], www.ltsn.ac.uk/genericcentre/docs/Critical%20review%20of%20assessme nt%20research.rtf

Entwistle, N. (1987), *Understanding classroom learning*. London: Hodder and Stoughton. Quoted in Entwistle, N. and Waterson, S. (1998), 'Approaches to Studying and Levels of Processing in University Students', *British journal of educational psychology*, 58, 258-265.

Entwistle, N. (1997), 'Contrasting perspectives on learning', in Marton, F., Hounsell, D., and Entwistle, N. (1997), *The Experience of Learning - implications for teaching and studying in higher education*. Edinburgh: Scottish Academic Press.

Entwistle, N. and Tait, H. (1990), 'Approaches to learning, evaluation of teaching, and preferences for contracting academic environments', *Higher education*, 19, 169-194.

Fuller, M. (2002), 'Assessment for real in Virtual Learning Environments – how far can we go?', Conference paper: *At the Interface - Virtual Learning and Higher Education*, Mansfield College, Oxford Available as: www.inter-disciplinary.net/Assessment_VLE.pdf

Garrett, D., Gilroy, P., Saxon, D. and Cairns, C. (2002), 'Are FE/HE staff ICT competent? A report from the tRISSt research project', in Banks, S., Goodyear, P., Hodgson, V. and McConnell, D. (eds.) *Networked Learning*

2002 - Proceedings of the Third International Conference. Sheffield: University of Sheffield.

Holland S. and Arrowsmith, A. (2000), 'Towards a productive assessment practice: Practising theory online', *Assessment and the expanded text consortium.* Newcastle: University of Northumbria.

Jenkins, M., Browne, T., and Armitage, S. (2001), *Management and implementation of Virtual Learning Environments.* UCISA. Available as www.ucisa.ac.uk/groups/tlig/vle/VLEsurvey.pdf

JM Consulting (2002), *Teaching and learning infrastructure in higher education – Report to the HEFCE.* HEFCE June 2002/31 [online]. www.hefce.ac.uk/Pubs/hefce/2002/02_31.htm

Kearsley, G. and Shneiderman, B. (1998), 'Engagement theory: A framework for technology-based teaching and learning', *Educational technology*, 38(5), 20-23.

Khakhar, D. (1999), 'A framework for open distance learning: organization and management', in van der Molen (ed.), *Virtual University?* London: Portland Press. 27-40. vu.portlandpress.com/pdf/vu_ch3.pdf

Lamb, J. (2002), 'Moving Inside the Virtual Classroom', *Financial Times, March 21 2002.*

Laurillard, D. (1993), *Rethinking university teaching - a framework for the effective use of educational technology.* London: Routledge.

Lave, J. (1988), *Cognition in practice.* Cambridge: Cambridge University Press.

Littlejohn, A. (2002), 'New lessons from past experiences: recommendations for improving continuing professional development in the use of ICT', *Journal of computer assisted learning*, 18

LTSN Generic Centre (2002), *Institutional learning and teaching strategies - Key themes and recommendation*, LTSN [online]. www.ltsn.ac.uk/genericcentre/projects/assessment/resources/ilts/

Maher, M.L., Simoff, S. and Clark, S. (2001), 'Learner-centred open virtual environments as places', in Dillenbourg, P., Eurelings, A. and Hakkarainen, K. (eds.), *Proceedings of the EuropeanPerspectives on Computer-Supported Collaborative Learning Conference,* 437-444.

Martin, A. (2001), *CITscapes Project - Report from phase 1 - Higher Education*, Glasgow: IT Education Unit. 9-10.

McGoldrick, C. (2002), *Creativity and curriculum design : what do academics think?* Commissioned Imaginative Research Study, LTSN June 2002. Availabel at: http://www.ltsn.ac.uk/genericcentre

Milligan, C. (1999), *Delivering Staff and Professional Development Using Virtual Learning Environments.* Edinburgh: Heriot-Watt. [online] www.jtap.ac.uk/reports/htm/jtap-044.html

MIT (2001), *MIT OpenCourseWare -- Fact Sheet.* MIT April 4th 2001. [online] web.mit.edu/newsoffice/nr/2001/ocw-facts.html

National Audit Office (2002a), *Widening participation in higher education in England.* The Stationary Office.
National Audit Office (2002b), *Improving student achievement in English Higher Education.* The Stationary Office.

Perry, S, (2002), *Stretching the IMS Specifications to Achieve Interoperability – The CO3 Project.* University of Wales Bangor: CeLT, ch 6 [online] cetis.bangor.ac.uk/co3/

Phillips, R. (1998), 'What research says about learning on the Internet', in McBeath, C., McLoughlin, C., and Atkinson, R. (eds.) *Planning for progress, partnership and profit. Proceedings EdTech'98.* Perth: Australian Society for Educational Technology.

Pring, R. (2001), *The Changing Nature of Universities: economic relevance, social inclusion or personal excellence.* Oxford: Institute for the Advancement of University Learning, [online]. www.learning.ox.ac.uk/iaul/ProfPring.pdf

Race, P.(2001), *A Briefing on Self, Peer & Group Assessment.* York: LTSN [online] www.ltsn.ac.uk/genericcentre/projects/assessment/assess_series/09SelfPeerGroup.pdf

Ramsey, C. (2002), 'Using Virtual Learning Environments to facilitate new learning relationships', *BEST 2002 Annual Conference, 8 –10 April 2002.* Edinburgh [online] www.business.ltsn.ac.uk/events/BEST%202002/Papers/c_ramsey.PDF

Raskin, J. (1994), *Intuitive equals familiar.* Communications of the ACM, 37(9), 17

Saroyan, A and Snell, L. (1997), 'Variations in lecturing styles', *Higher education*, 33, 85-104.

Simpson, W., Evans, D., Ely, R. and Stiles, M. (2002), 'Findings from the HEI 'flip' project: 1. Application issues', *International journal of continuing engineering education and life-long learning* (In Press)

Smith, T. (2002), *Strategic factors affecting the uptake, in higher education, of new and emerging technologies for learning and teaching.* York: Technologies   Centre,   [online] www.techlearn.ac.uk/NewDocs/HEDriversFinal.rtf

Stiles, M. (2000a), 'Developing tacit and codified knowledge and subject culture within a Virtual Learning Environment', *IJEEE*, 37(1), 13-25.

Stiles, M. (2000b), 'Effective Learning and the Virtual Learning Environment', in: *EUNIS 2000: Towards virtual universities.* Poznan: Instytut Informatyki Politechniki Poznanskiej. 171-180.

Stiles, M. (2001a), *Briefing Paper No 5 - Pedagogy and Virtual Learning Environment (VLE) evaluation and selection.* JISC, [online] www.jisc.ac.uk/mle/reps/briefings/bp5.pdf

Stiles, M. (2001b), *SURF Consortium: Interoperability between COSE and MIS systems used across the consortium.* Staffordshire University: COSE Project, [online] www.jisc.ac.uk/mle/interop/rtfs/rep-surf.pdf

Stiles, M. (2002), 'Staying on the Track', *JISC Inform*, 1, 4-8.

Stiles, M. and Orsmond, P. (2002), 'Managing Active Student Learing with a Virtual Learning Environment', in: Fallows, S. and Bhanhot, R. (eds.) *Educational development through information and communications technologies.* Kogan Press.

Thomson, A. (2002), 'Poor not needed to reach 50% target, Hodge admits', *The Times Higher Education Supplement*, 8 February 2002.

Tomes, N. and Higgeson, C. (1998), *Exploring the Network for Teaching and Learning in Scottish Higher Education.* Edinburgh: Herriot-Watt. Available as: www.talisman.hw.ac.uk/tna/

Vygotsky, L. (1978), *Mind in Society*. Cambridge MA: Cambridge University Press.

Warren, D. (2002), 'Curriculum design in a context of widening participation in Higher Education', *Arts and humanities in Higher Education*, 1(1), 85-99.

Wilson, S. (2002), *Experts question SCORM's pedagogic value*. University of Wales Bangor: CETIS [online] www.cetis.ac.uk/content/20020802112525/printArticle

Woodrow, M. and Yorke, M. (2002), *Social Class and Participation*. Universities UK: UUK Publications.

Young, Z and Morris, H. (2000), *An holistic approach to the use of labour market intelligence (LMI) in HE strategy planning, DfEE HEQE LMI Project Final Report*. Manchester: UMIST. Available as: www.lmi4he.ac.uk/Documents/finalreport.doc.

Assessment for Real in Virtual Learning Environments - How Far Can We Go?

Mike Fuller

Abstract

The use of tests is a common feature of Virtual Learning Environments (VLEs). Assessment tools in VLEs have frequently been regarded as limited to the reinforcement of basic skills and the lower levels of the cognitive domain. However the resource pressures that have lead to larger classes and to the use of VLEs also apply - perhaps particularly apply - to assessment.

This chapter takes an overview of the potential, as well as the problems, of assessing students' learning using the tools of VLEs, so as to make cost-effective use of staff time. To what extent are the perceived weaknesses and limitations of assessment in a VLE inherent? Or with imagination and further development can we go beyond them? How far up the cognitive hierarchy can we go?

The chapter reviews the use of VLEs for assessment. Although informed by the author's experience in using a VLE for assessing business students' knowledge and understanding of quantitative methods, the chapter takes a broader, interdisciplinary perspective.

The conclusion is that while there are inherent limitations in the specific assessment tools of a VLE, there is underexploited potential for the resource-effective use of VLEs in a variety of assessment tasks in ways that develop rather than merely record student learning.

Consideration of the potential scope of VLEs for assessment raises some questions about Bloom's taxonomy of the cognitive domain (Bloom et al, 1956). This consideration leads towards a perspective in which at the highest levels of the hierarchy *Synthesis* can be seen as more demanding than *Evaluation*. This is the reverse of the original ordering.

1.   Computers and Assessment

Virtual Learning Environments (VLEs) provide a range of facilities for delivering a module online, supplementing or replacing traditional modes of delivery. A VLE will typically provide *curriculum mapping*, structuring the curriculum into assessable components and a means of *delivery* of the module with additional links to external *learning resources*. There will also be facilities for: electronic *communication* between tutors and learners and between learners; provision of *tutor support* to learners; *tracking* of student participation and performance; support of online *assessment* (JISC, 2001; Erskine, 2003).

The facilities provided by a VLE in practice allow the replication of traditional assessment methods online. Essays and other assignments can be submitted electronically, marked individually and returned to students with comments. Materials developed by course participants for presentations can be made available to fellow students through student web pages within the module's VLE which can provide links to documents in other formats such as PowerPoint presentations.

In addition, marks for assessed work can be recorded within the VLE. Depending on the facilities of the institution's student information systems, assessment marks recorded at the module level may be automatically transferred to departmental or institutional level without rekeying. Institutions that provide well integrated facilities for providing online information about programmes, modules and assessment results in which VLEs for individual modules are embedded can be said to provide a Managed Learning Environment (MLE). (The Joint Information Systems Committee (JISC) ISC Briefing Paper 1 provides a summary overview of MLEs and how VLEs are embedded in them (JISC, 2001).) An interesting institutional case study of the introduction of computer based assessment across the University of Luton is given by Steven and Zakrzewski (Steven and Zakrzewski, 2002).

However VLEs provide additional opportunities for computer based assessment. Tests can be set and assessed automatically if the format of the questions allows for this. Multiple choice answers can be provided or short answers parsed to see if they conform to a permitted pattern of answer, perhaps written as a 'regular expression' as in WebCT, for example. From this author's experience this process can be time consuming. AutoMark software on the other hand uses information extraction methods to create more robust computerised marking of free-text answers to open-ended questions (Mitchell et al, 2002). In disciplines with a quantitative element, the answers to calculated questions can be checked to see if they are accurate enough to be accepted. Feedback to students can be provided. This can even respond to the student's individual answers. The choice of questions presented to any student can be varied by selecting questions at random from a larger set. Generating such sets of questions is conceptually easier for calculated questions that just change the parameter values in an equation than it is for short answer and multiple choice questions.

The development of such sets of questions is inevitably more time consuming than that spent creating assessments in a traditional learning environment. The development time for online assessment questions means that it is sensible to support the creation of databanks of questions for each discipline in order to share the load. White and Thomas discuss issues involved in doing this. Practical issues such as the difficulty of transferring from one VLE to another, and the fact that assessment in higher education is still largely paper-based suggest to them the need to focus on simple types of question that can be moved more easily and work in paper as well as online (White and Thomas, 2000). This prescription is very limiting however. It would be helpful for more work to be done to enable the more complex forms of questions that can be marked automatically, such as short answer questions and calculated questions, to be moved more easily between different VLEs.

However, once created, automated assessment means that the assessments of large student groups can be marked virtually simultaneously, giving rapid turnaround with prompt feedback. For large modules the marking time saved can more than compensate for the time creating the assessment. The facilities for automatically recording marks also make it easier to manage the subdivision of the assessment into shorter components. This also improves the feedback on learning.

For example, in two modules taught by the author with about 180 postgraduate and 300 undergraduate students respectively in 2002-03, each paper-based coursework assessment covering 6 or 8 weeks' work was replaced by four short online components. Now the work done in weeks 1 and 2 has a short assessment with a deadline a week or two later. Feedback on this is given within a day or two of the deadline. Previously, assessment of this material would have been part of a larger assignment with a deadline 6 or 7 weeks later. This would have required individual marking, adding to the time taken before students receive feedback on the topics. If assessment is to be genuinely and usefully formative then reducing the time between the learning and the feedback on that learning is beneficial.

Increasing experience with online assessment of this kind has pushed this author towards shortening the time between completing the lectures and classes about a topic and the deadline for the related assessment component. Initially two weeks were allowed for this gap. However, many students leave doing the work until the deadline is only a day or two away. With highly sequential units, as most quantitative methods and other technical modules typically are, each week builds on the previous weeks' work. Learning of the current material can be impeded if the previous material has not been mastered. For this reason, I have moved to shortening the time between teaching a topic (usually taking a week or two) and assessing it, nearer to one week rather than two. This means that feedback is provided to students earlier too.

In the trade off between the largely fixed costs of developing questions for online assessment and the time savings from avoiding individual marking, there must be some break even point at which the time savings in marking offset the development time. If a traditional assessment takes 15 minutes to mark, the marking time for an assessment taken by 100 students is 25 hours. With automated marking some sampling of answers is needed for the developer of the assessment to assure that the templates for acceptable answers with short-answer questions does what was intended. This still leaves substantial time for developing the questions, if you cannot find or buy in suitable questions from elsewhere. However, learning to use the facilities of most VLEs itself takes time. During this learning phase at least, the break even point at which use of online automated assessment is justified is probably a module size of about 100 students. If the module developer has more experience of using online assessment or if more use is to be made of assessment tools developed elsewhere, the break even point will come at a rather smaller module size.

One feature of this trade off is that the time spent on designing questions comes up front while marking time comes later in the module. If you are considering making a switch from traditional to online assessment it is important to recognise this and plan for it.

To make significant savings in marking time, the marking has to be 'automated' in the sense that software checks students' answers to see if they are acceptable or not. Clearly we cannot automate essay marking, though short answers of a few words can be compared with a template of acceptable answers. Such questions are more awkward to develop than multiple choice questions but provide greater flexibility.

Because of this background, computer-aided assessment is often seen as synonymous with 'objective testing'. A criticism sometimes advanced of such forms of assessment is that they are limited to the reinforcement of basic skills and the lower levels of the cognitive domain. In the sense that questions suitable for automated marking clearly cannot test the skills of organising and presenting material in extended form that an essay, project or even an examination answer can, this is clearly true. However the question arises – just how far can we take online assessment with automated marking?

2.   Bloom's Taxonomy and Assessment

The taxonomy of competences within the cognitive domain developed by Benjamin Bloom's committee of examiners is well known with its hierarchy rising from Knowledge, Comprehension and Application to what McGrath and Noble see as the higher order thinking of Analysis, Synthesis and Evaluation (Bloom et al, 1956; McGrath and Noble, 1993). To what extent can these various levels within the hierarchy be tested with questions suitable for automated marking? Are we stuck with the lower levels of Bloom's hierarchy?

Evidence from a range of subjects suggests we are not. Ken Masters and his colleagues at the University of Cape Town have created a very useful site on designing and managing multiple choice questions that includes an appendix linking this to Bloom's taxonomy (Masters et al, 1999, Appendix C). This has examples of multiple choice questions testing at five of the six levels – only synthesis is omitted. How is Synthesis to be tested?

3.   Assessing Knowledge, Comprehension and Application
        Let us start with examples of assessing Knowledge, Comprehension and Application. In teaching about the management of information to business students, a useful tool is Deming's Wheel, which outlines a cycle of *Planning, Doing, Checking* and *Acting* in which ideas for improvement are tested scientifically in these four stages in which a modification to a process is planned, together with how we will judge its results, the planned change is implemented, the consequences are monitored and conclusions are drawn. (Deming actually attributes the oringinal idea to Walter Shewhart (Deming, 1986).) From the knowledge gained, or because new problems have emerged, further ideas for improving business processes are tested using the same cycle.
        If we ask, "What is the name given to the cycle of Planning, Doing, Checking and Acting used in the analysis and improvement of business processes?" then we can give a number of answers, of which Deming's Wheel would be one. If students choose this answer, they have demonstrated Knowledge. As Masters and his colleagues say, too many questions of this kind would reduce assessment to Trivial Pursuit!

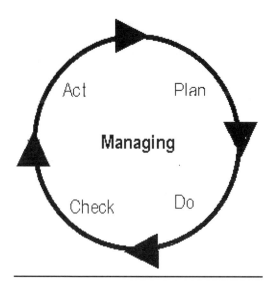

Figure 1. Deming's Wheel

If students are asked to identify which of four brief descriptions of activities corresponds to the Checking stage then choosing the one that talks about "Monitoring the consequences of a change to a business process" will demonstrate Comprehension.

Suppose however we provide a short contextual paragraph:
Fair Trade International is considering introducing a new organic coffee for filter machines. The company commission Fuller Research Services to undertake market research with existing customers to assess whether they would be prepared to pay extra for an organic product.

The student is then asked "What stage of Deming's Wheel does this best correspond to?" If they choose Planning, they have demonstrated Application. To answer this correctly they need not only to have comprehended the relevant knowledge but they need also to be able to apply it.

In a subject like quantitative methods, calculated questions will also frequently provide another type of question that tests Application.

4.   Assessing Analysis, Synthesis and Evaluation

The use of contextual material provides a way of moving assessment even further up the scale. However, the context should be one with which the student can be expected to be familiar and its language should be comprehensible to those for whom the language of education and assessment is a second language.

For example the following question might reasonably be said to go beyond simple Application and require the demonstration of Analysis since the range of issues raised about survey quality is wide.

A city newspaper has a circulation of about 10,000 in an area with a population of 400,000. It wants to find out what residents think about shopping facilities in the city, and encloses a questionnaire in the paper which readers are asked to complete and return to the newspaper's offices. 1,000 replies are received, 70% of which are from women.
Tick the boxes [not shown here] for which you think the accompanying statements apply.
1. The population from which the sample is drawn is not the relevant one for the purpose described.
2. The response rate is low.

3. There will be a high rate of response errors in the survey.

4. The survey does not use a random sample.

5. Tick this box if you think it would be bad for the quality of the survey if one of the city's big department stores sponsored the survey with a large advertisement near the questionnaire. Leave this box blank if you think the idea is a good one.

Full marks are given to those who tick all the boxes except 3.

Assessing Synthesis using any of the approaches to automated questions seems to be beyond their scope. Synthesis involves assembling parts to create a new whole so it is therefore not possible to reduce its assessment to a series of short-answer questions. One possibility would be to adapt the approach Masters and others have recommended for assessing Evaluation. This is to present a "student's answer" to an appropriate question and to ask respondents to judge the quality of the answer. However this would not assess students' ability to create a good synthesis in answering a question. It would only their ability to evaluate whether an answer provided a good synthesis or not. This aspect of the cognitive domain is the most difficult to assess using computer-based automated marking. This point is developed further in the next section.

Assessing Evaluation using the mock answer approach is more practicable. For example consider the following question, designed to evaluate students' understanding of some aspects of hypothesis testing:

A national survey has suggested that 45% of all households in the country have a personal computer (PC). In Stourminster, in a random sample of 20 households, 14 have a PC. Students were asked to analyse this situation using the ideas of hypothesis testing and to illustrate the concepts of the null and alternative hypotheses, probvalues, size of test and appropriate decisions for 5% and 1% tests. This is one of the answers. Evaluate the answer using one of the evaluations given below.

'The binomial distribution is relevant to this context. Tables of the distribution show that the probability of 13 or fewer households in a sample of 20 having a PC is 0.9786, so the probability of 14 or more households in the sample of 20 having a PC is 0.0214.

As the probvalue of the sample data is 0.0214, if we tested the null hypothesis that the national proportion of

45% applies to Stourminster against the alternative hypothesis that the proportion of all households in Stourminster having a PC is more than 45% we would reject the null hypothesis at a 5% size of test but retain it at a 1% size of test. Because the alternative hypothesis only considers change in one direction, this is an example of a one tailed test.'

How would you judge this student's answer?

1. EXCELLENT (all points correct in an appropriate order with clear and correct explanations)

2. GOOD (all points correct in an appropriate order but the explanations are not as clear as they should be).

3. MEDIOCRE (one or two required elements are missing OR the answer uses in an inappropriate order, OR the explanations are not clear OR the explanations are irrelevant)

4. UNACCEPTABLE (more than two elements are missing AND the order is inappropriate AND the explanations are not clear AND/OR irrelevant)

The grading criteria adapt those of Masters. In fact this is at least a good answer and arguably excellent, depending on the view taken about how much explanation is needed.

With ingenuity then, online questions for automated marking can be formulated that assess most levels of Bloom's taxonomy. There are also statistical methods for assessing the effectiveness of questions (Masters et al, 1999, section 4.6).

5.   Ordering Synthesis and Evaluation in Bloom's Hierarchy

With ingenuity we can provide, using the approach of the previous section, questions that could be marked automatically which assess Evaluation. But is it possible to assess Synthesis in this way?

The suggestion here is that Evaluation can at least to some extent be assessed in terms of the ability to recognise a good or a less good evaluation. The more I consider the issue, the more convinced I have become that we cannot assess the ability to synthesise through asking students to recognise the quality in the writing of others. In a very fundamental sense, Synthesis involves the internalisation of learning and the ability to express a network of internalised, interrelated ideas in one's own words.

This leads to the thought that this creative aspect of Synthesis is not merely an insuperable impediment to finding automated forms of assessment for it. In almost all forms of knowledge, learning is not static but dynamic. Subject benchmarks may at best capture what is most relevant for an area of study at a point of time. No one expects them to remain unchanged as the world changes and as research and scholarship bring new insights. The ability to be a good evaluator will be important in assessing the quality of the foundations and structure of a subject but the ability to build new and better structures of knowledge also requires development. Synthesis is fundamental to this.

Arguably then, we should see Synthesis as being at the top of this hierarchy, rather than Evaluation. If we want to assess it, we must move outside the realm of automated assessment tools.

6.   Using VLEs for Other Forms of Assessment

Because of the unavoidable limitations inherent in automated marking, it is unlikely that most modules in most programmes will judge that all their learning objectives can be assessed in this way. It is therefore useful to consider how VLEs can enhance other approaches to assessment.

One aspect of VLEs that can be harnessed for the task is the ability for students to present materials in web pages or in resources linked to web pages. This provides an alternative to the live, face-to-face, form of presentation. Where local assessment rules require either two staff to be present or that presentations assessed by a single individual be videotaped, presentations are sometimes seen as expensive forms of assessment in resource terms. Student presentations where the materials remain accessible in the VLE overcome some of these objections. Because they are also accessible to fellow students on the module, they also provide opportunities for students to assess, at least informally and perhaps formally, the work of their peers. This process gives students an insight into the assessment of their own work and it can thus be used as a tool of formative assessment.

The communications facilities of VLEs also provide opportunities for documenting and assessing participation in online discussion. If online discussion partly or completely replaces face-to-face seminars, participation in seminars no longer needs to be synchronous. Contributions to discussions also remain available and, if necessary, assessment of online contributions to discussion can be reviewed later in a way that participation in face-to-face seminars cannot.

Additionally, as pointed out in Section 1, written forms of assessment, provided they are produced using electronic means, can all be handled within a VLE. In some contexts it can be helpful to ask for assignments to be submitted both online in a VLE and also on paper. This reduces the possibility of assessments in a large module being mislaid. One copy is always available within the VLE.

Because the VLE can only handle electronic documents, there are some resource and skills development implications. Printed documents, even when predominantly word-processed, are often annotated by hand to include unusual characters from foreign languages or to add equations or diagrams.

For the VLE submission there can be no annotation by hand so if they wish to include a hand-drawn diagram it is important to provide students with access to a scanner and training in using software to create diagrams and charts electronically. For relevant modules, some training in using an equation editor within a word-processed document is needed and fonts are required that provide foreign language or other specialist characters.

6.   Conclusions

VLEs provide a range of opportunities for assessment that can work for most levels of Bloom's cognitive hierarchy using questions suitable for automated marking. The development costs are substantial and it makes economic sense to pool resources but the time savings for large modules are substantial.

It seems that within Bloom's hierarchy the assessment of the ability to synthesise is beyond the scope of automated assessment tools. Here we are not looking just for specific content but at the way concepts, evidence and argument are combined by learners after they have internalised an area of study. This needs a longer piece of work that could not practicably be marked against a template of acceptable answers.

With sufficient ingenuity assessment tools can be automated for other levels of Bloom's taxonomy.

There is a strong case for discipline-based learning and teaching support networks such as those created within Higher Education in the United Kingdom to act as repositories for tested banks of questions which staff (but not their students) can access to create module assessments.

VLEs also provide other opportunities for assessment that, while not automatic, may save some staff time or provide evidence that enables assessed material to be reviewed later if necessary.

References

Bloom, B.S., Englehart, M.D., Furst E.J. and Krathwohl D.R., (1956), *Taxonomy of Educational Objectives: The Classification of Educational Goals, Handbook I: Cognitive Domain.* New York: Longman.

Deming, W.E., (1986), *Out of the Crisis.* New York: Wiley.

Erskine, J., (2003). *Glossary of Key VLE Related Terms.* [online] http://www.hlst.ltsn.ac.uk/projects/specialists/erskine_glossary.html [Accessed 11 April 2003].

JISC (Joint Information Systems Committee) (2001), *JISC MLE and VLE Briefing Papers.* [online] http://www.jisc.ac.uk/mle/reps/briefings/ [Accessed 11 April 2003].

Masters, K., Delpierre, G. and Carneson, J. (1999), *Designing and Managing Multiple Choice Questions.* [online] http://www.uct.ac.za/projects/cbe/mcqman/mcqman01.html [Accessed 11 April 2003].

McGrath, H., and Noble, T. (1993), *Different kids same classroom: Making mixed ability classes really work..* Melbourne: Longman.

Mitchell, T., Russell, T., Broomhead, P. and Aldridge, N. (2002), *Towards Robust Computerised Marking of Free-Text Responses,* presented to the CAA Conference at Loughborough University. [online] http://www.lboro.ac.uk/service/ltd/flicaa/conf2002/pdfs/Mitchell_t1.pdf [Accessed 11 April 2003].

Steven, C., and Zakrzewski, S. (2002), 'Student assessment using ICT', in: Fallows, S. and Bhanot, R. (eds.) *Educational Development through Information and Communications Technology.* London: Kogan Page, 123-132.

White, S., and Thomas, H. (2000), *Creating large-scale test banks: a briefing for participative discussions of issues and agendas,* presented to the CAA Conference at Loughborough University. [online] http://www.lboro.ac.uk/service/ltd/flicaa/conf2000/pdfs/whites.pdf [Accessed 11 April 2003].

Part III

Looking Before Leaping:
Issues In Virtual Higher Education

C.P. Snow Revisited: The Two Cultures of Faculty and Administration

James Wood

Abstract

Over forty years ago, C.P. Snow warned that the gulf between two academic cultures was getting so wide that they could not easily communicate with each other, to the detriment of public interest (Snow, 1959). The two cultures he described were those of the "literary intellectuals" and the scientists. Today there is a similar gulf, but this time between the faculty, including both literary intellectuals as well as scientists, and the university administration. It will be argued in this chapter that the faculty has maintained a commitment to outstanding teaching and scholarship, along with community service, whereas the university administration has increasingly devised 'strategic plans' for the university stressing other, often quite different, goals, particularly stressing the financial bottom line and more generally the business model as a central goal for the university.

With administrators increasingly focused on cutting costs and the faculty remaining interested in providing quality higher education, a tension, or dialectic, was built into university relationships during the 1990s that continues today and does not augur well for higher education and the public it serves. This chapter will outline a series of these strategic university plans that I feel, if continued in their present form, will greatly undermine this most pivotal of social institutions.

Higher education in the 1990s was characterised by multiple crises, difficulties, and strategic planning schemes created by administrators often quite removed from university classrooms and sites of research. Distance learning schemes have become prototypical of other kinds of controversial, bottom-line-oriented, strategic plans. 'Strategic planning' is a term, borrowed from business and lately used by university administrators, which refers to broad-scale future plans for organisations and often entailing anticipated large changes, similar to the major downsizing of corporations in the 1990s. 'Leadership teams' in organisations are often assigned the duties of initiating these strategic plans, usually guided by top-down assumptions involving little or no consultation with the groups most affected by these changes.

This chapter will address three related questions:

1. What were the strategic plans that affect higher education in the 1990s?
2. What are the problems for higher education they are creating?

3.   Is there evidence of faculty and student awareness of these problems, and a willingness to politically organise to deal with them?

Most of the empirical references will be to situations in the United States and California (Wood and Valenzuela, 1996; Wood and Valenzuela, 1997; Finkin, 1996; American Association of University Professors, 1993; American Sociological Association, 1997). However there is much evidence, such as the essays in the internationally-focused book edited by Gerard J. DeGroot, *Student Protest: The Sixties and After*, as well as the Special Issue of *Sociological Perspectives* on "The Academy Under Siege," and several issues between 1998 and 2001 of *The Chronicle of Higher Education's* International section, that at least some of America's university problems are shared by other countries such as Germany, South Korea, India, South Africa, Mexico, China, Kazakhstan, Romania, El Salvador, France, Britain and Australia (DeGroot, 1998; Hohm and Wood, 1998). It is also my belief that common solutions can be found, as discussed in *Sociological Perspectives* (Wood, 1998a). For those countries or universities not yet afflicted by such difficulties, it may be useful to see the warning signs elsewhere in order to enable faster response to the problems if they occur in the future.

1.   Distance Learning as a Strategic Plan
Although other authors in this book and elsewhere use different definitions, distance learning for this chapter involves the use of modern computer technology to transmit higher education from a central location to many students in front of computer or television screens at physical distances from the academic point of origin. A conference in Sonoma, California, keynoted by an administrator from the UK's Open University, purported to show participants how to teach 5,000 students per class section.

To indicate the increasing use of distance learning in higher education, the following institutions have initiated distance education programs: Open University in the UK, UCLA with its THEN (The Higher Education Network) program (re-named OnLineLearning.net), CETI (the California Education Technology Initiative) of the California State University (CSU) system (which collapsed), the California Virtual University (CVU) which includes universities and colleges throughout California (which also collapsed), the Western Governors University (WGU) which includes several entire university systems throughout the Western United States except California, Michael Milken's Knowledge Universe and, probably the most well known of them all, University of Phoenix (see Brent Muirhead's chapter in this volume). This is only a partial list and does not include the American corporations initiating distance learning programs leading to degrees and certificates but it does reflect a new direction of higher education that requires serious evaluation (Marchese, 1998).

I first heard of distance learning as a proposed solution to presumed system-wide higher educational problems in 1990 through discussions by the California State University Chancellor's Office about the supposed upcoming lack of Ph.D.s to properly teach students in the CSU system. Given the large numbers of Ph.D.s in the United States and in California alone, this seemed odd to me and to my colleagues, who were unaware of any such looming crisis. It seemed that other agendas were involved when the administrators argued about the need to install widespread and costly technology throughout the 20-plus campus system to teach students at a physical distance from college classrooms. In particular, it appeared that the corporations selling this expensive hardware and software would be the ones to particularly gain by CSU and other universities instituting distance learning on a wide scale and not the students at whom such an education was aimed.

Over the years my suspicions about distance learning have unfortunately been realised. Microsoft, GTE, Fujitsu, and Hughes Electronics, along with the California State University system, were part of a multi-year, multi-million dollar scheme involving computer hardware, software and the marketing of distance learning courses. Due to many financing problems, and potential legal monopoly problems, the California Education Technology Initiative collapsed after two years of backstage negotiations of which few faculty staff were even aware. While many faculty and students - and even campus administrators - breathed a sigh of relief when this unwieldy plan folded, they were soon to learn about an attempt to revive such a plan with most of the previous drawbacks, but without consultation of the groups most affected, namely students and faculty. This new scheme was labelled Son of CETI, with all the pejorative implications of that phrase, but it, too, has apparently been de-emphasised. Yet there are real differences between faculty and administration regarding these issues, with one administrator even referring to unjustified faculty angst, a position with which many faculty strongly disagree (Ingram, 1999, B-10).

What is wrong with distance learning as a general approach to providing quality higher education? Professors and students have commented on the key differences between distance learning and in-class instruction, including an eloquent discussion by Jerry Farber (1998). Farber showed the many benefits of classroom interchanges and stimulation including growth in intellectual breadth and flexibility and the advantage of personal inspiration that contact with professors can provide which are impossible to similarly obtain through computer screens. Other commentators have focused on the high drop-out rate of distance learners as compared to those in classrooms, the inability of professors to really know if those taking distance education examinations are the students receiving grades and diplomas and the tendency toward making universities merely "Digital Diploma Mills", David Noble's colorful term for distance learning (Noble, 1998a; Noble, 1998b).

Distance learning as a general way to provide higher education is problematical because, in addition to the loss of intellectual stimulation and inspiration that can come from classroom interactions, it is part of a much larger scheme to transform and, in my view, diminish higher education. This point is essentially unknown to the American and international public. Since decisions now being quietly made will significantly affect the general public, these decisions require considerable evaluation and debate, the type of debate sponsored by the Faculty Coalition for Public Higher Education (FCPHE, 1999).

2.   Related Strategic Plans

Distance learning fits into a series of strategic plans developed by university administrators who are attempting to re-focus higher education on the following issues:

1.   'Learning instead of teaching', whereby learning from a physical distance is the model - with this view often coming from the same administrators who call for better teaching

2.   'Outcomes assessment' of learning, particularly the use of standardised, multiple-choice testing procedures devised by off-campus commercial agencies quite removed from college classrooms, similar to the organisations that produce tests like the Scholastic Aptitude Test (SAT) and the Graduate Record Examination (GRE) for mass distribution to distance learning (or in-class) students. This view often comes from the same administrators who call for better writing from students

3.   The commercialisation of the university whereby businesses are to play much larger and direct roles in universities than ever before while making large profits from universities, students, professors and even alumni (this was the aim of the California Education Technology Initiative from a business standpoint)

4.   The related commodification of higher education whereby 'products' (courses) are 'purchased' (through distance learning) for 'consumption' (obtaining a Digital Diploma Mill degree)

5.   The loss of professors' intellectual property rights over the courses they teach to maximise profits for others

6.   The increasing reliance on underpaid part-time instructors instead of full-time, tenured faculty (part-time instruction has increased to over 40% for many American universities to the detriment of students who need fully professional and committed faculty who will be around later to write them letters of recommendation for jobs and graduate school)

7.   The attacks on tenure which could greatly undermine the academic freedom necessary for universities to continue producing the great innovations in science, the economy and technology itself (Finkin, 1996)

8.   The increasing control over universities by administrators who favor an imperial approach to higher education that stresses the above connected tendencies

9.   The lessening control by departments when faculty hiring is based on administrative plans instead of departmental curricular needs

10.   The gradual elimination, or at least significant weakening, of targeted departments by administrative refusal to hire tenure-track faculty for any purpose.

Higher education will be continually diminished if these trends are not soon reversed. Indeed, there is a negative dynamic already under way. Bright younger scholars who had planned on having an academic career are now re-thinking this career choice. If the only work available to those who have to spend the greater part of a decade in graduate school arduously preparing themselves to become professors is non-tenured, lowly paid part-time instruction delivered by distance learning, then who is going to bother? Several of my own university colleagues have indicated they no longer plan to encourage their children to become professors because of the rapidly declining state of American higher education. In his jarring poem of the 1950s, *Howl*, Allen Ginsberg indicated that the greatest minds of his generation were being lost to madness (Ginsberg, 1959). The greatest minds of the current generation may not be lost to madness, but they surely will be lost to higher education if these trends are not reversed.

It is apparent that in the post-war years American higher education has played a central role in the U.S. attaining its powerful position in the world. This has certainly been the case in California with its many world-class, universities and colleges.

The widely read report on American education, *A Nation at Risk*, warned that public high school education was being organised as if by a foreign enemy (The National Commission on Excellence in Education, 1983). Since the 1990s, public higher education in America has been similarly treated, as if organized by the same foreign enemy out to destroy this essential institution which strengthens all other American institutions, from the economy to the arts and sciences through to government, and which makes economic mobility and improvement in life-styles possible for millions of Americans. The current, unrelenting attacks on American higher education, including the imposition of distance learning schemes, if not prevented by those in power, will significantly weaken this pivotal institution.

3.   **Recommendations and Solutions**
        What is the solution to all of this? Now is the time for the public
to insist on restoring higher education by reversing these negative trends
begun in the 1990s, and returning the university to its previous position of
strength and dedicated public service. The public should insist to elected
officials on the passage of laws requiring a large majority of in-class
instruction instead of a majority (or all) distance learning classes for
college and university degrees. This is consistent with the view of the
university accrediting agency, the Western Association of Schools and
Colleges (WASC) which limits the number of distance learning courses
acceptable for college degrees. These laws should cover: the protection of
the intellectual property rights of faculty staff over their courses; the
requirement that there are substantial numbers of full-time, tenure-track
faculty instead of part-time instructors; the strengthening of tenure, which
is at the base of academic freedom required to produce great discoveries
and innovations; the mandating of minimum levels of national and state
budgets dedicated to public higher education to avoid major disruptions in
economic recessions; and the prevention of corporate takeovers and
privatisation of, or undue private influence upon, public higher education.
These and similar laws would go a long way toward supporting higher
education against the current onslaught which, if left unchecked, will
damage it beyond recognition.

4.   **Evidence of Political Awareness and Responses to Issues**
        In the face of all the difficulties facing universities is there
evidence that university faculty staff and students have become aware of
the problems and begun to politically organise? In fact, there have been
conscious responses to these varied problems throughout the 1990s,
registering some successes, with more responses likely as the attacks
continue in this 21st century. Indeed, one of the most dramatic responses
was a successful faculty strike of several months at York University in
Canada over a proposed distance learning scheme that would have
drastically worsened faculty working conditions. This strike was led by
David Noble of Digital Diploma Mills fame. Ultimately the faculty secured
significant contractual control over the introduction of instructional
technology at York University after this protracted conflict (Noble, 1998a).
        Faculty members in the UK staged a nationwide strike over higher
wages in May of 1999 (*The Chronicle of Higher Education*, June 4, 1999:
A49). Though only of one day duration, the Association of University
Teachers (AUT) indicated this will be simply the first of several such job
actions to achieve their demands. This indeed may indicate heightened
faculty struggle in the UK to redress the diminished position of the faculty
created by the Conservative government of former Prime Minister
Margaret Thatcher which resulted in the negative trend described by AUT

Research Officer Stephen Court: "[t]he dominant employment trend in UK higher education is the casualisation of academic staff which is inevitably accompanied by growing job insecurity among staff in a climate of real-terms cuts in public funding" (Court, 1998, 772). This century may see a reversal in fortune for UK faculty if the strike portends of things to come.

One of the earliest responses to attacks on universities came in 1992 at San Diego State University where I had the misfortune of witnessing the then President of SDSU, Thomas Day, attempt to eliminate nine academic departments and terminate 111 tenured faculty and 35 tenure-track faculty virtually overnight. The American Association of University Professors indicated that this was the worst such occurrence in U.S. history (American Association of University Professors, 1993).

After recovering from the initial shock of this unprecedented administrative action, the faculty and students at San Diego State mounted a campaign of several months that eventually restored all departments and faculty staff and led to the dismissal of the President, his Vice President, and several Deans (Wood, 1998b; Ristine, 1995; e-mail public announcements at SDSU, 1997). This scenario was actually preceded by a surprisingly similar set of circumstances and results at Yale University (Bernstein, 1992). A few years later, the University of Minnesota experienced a similar attempt to significantly 'restructure' it, but a strong faculty response helped restore the university (Magner, 1997; Leik, 1998).

The actions by the faculty staff at San Diego State were also preceded by political actions by a committed group of San Diego State students which became known as the *Vigil*. The Vigil was a group unexpectedly formed by sociology undergraduate student Deborah Katz, two days after the announced departmental eliminations and faculty layoffs (Wood, 1998b). At a large public rally that she helped organise, she announced that she would remain outside the President's office around the clock for 120 days (which was the period before the negative decisions were to be enforced). After learning she was serious about this plan of action against the ensuing disaster, several other students offered to watch her books while she got a sleeping bag and then joined her sleeping in front of the President's Office. In fact, this protest continued for six months instead of the originally planned four months, with the students remaining outside the President's Office and Library until Election Day in November 1992. This was one of relatively few protests in which the protesters lived outdoors at the site of protest for long periods of time; the sucessful 1980s women's protest against nuclear misslies at Greenham Common in England being an obvious parallel (Cook and Kirk, 1984; Wood, 1998b). Since it quickly became clear that the San Diego State students were not going to suffer such losses to their education silently, this protest inspired many of those faculty staff and students who initially felt it was useless to fight back.

In addition to initiating a series of non-violent, non-institutionalised protests, the Vigil also initiated a major voter registration campaign throughout California, eventually obtaining 8,000 new registered student voters. This, in turn, inspired a student voter registration campaign two years later which signed up 4,000 new voters at San Diego State alone. Several close political races locally were probably influenced in favor of the pro-higher education candidates, as San Diego emerged with the state legislative delegation most favorable to higher education in California. Two of the members of the delegation, Steve Peace and Denise Moreno Ducheny, later headed the powerful state Senate and Assembly budget committees that greatly influence higher education financial allocations, and another member, Dede Alpert, became the head of the state Senate Education Committee. Higher education has greatly benefitted from their support.

In parallel to these efforts, a national graduate student lobby was organised out of Washington, D.C. that effectively lobbied for college student issues such as scholarship, grant, and student loan funding, as well as funding for higher education generally. The graduate students used computer technology such as e-mail to communicate with each other nationally about the problems facing higher education as well as recommended solutions to the problems. Indeed, the attacks on students are as devastating as attacks on faculty and departments, as witnessed by former House of Representatives Speaker Newt Gingrich's attempt to cut $11 billion from higher education, especially from funding college students, in a proposed mid-1990s federal budget (Wood and Valenzuela, 1996; Wood and Valenzuela, 1997). Yet the actions of the graduate students nationally helped reverse this proposed major budget cut to higher education.

In the spring of 1999 the faculty of the California State University system, representing approximately 20,000 faculty, rejected by a vote of 57% to 43% a proposed contract that would have institutionalised many of the negative issues discussed here, especially a centralisation of administrative control over the faculty (one of the main sources of the supposedly unjustified angst noted above) (Selingo, 1999; e-mail public announcements from CFA, 1999; Evans, 1999). It was not until this centralising tendency was mitigated and faculty control increased that a contract was finally approved by better than an 80% to 20% vote (e-mail public announcements from CFA, 1999; *Los Angeles Times*, 1999). While more analysis will be forthcoming on these votes of the largest university system in America, early analyses point to the fight against administrative control. This in turn was inspired by other recent union victories among such groups as the United Parcel Service workers, which launched a very successful strike against the large-scale expansion of part-time employees at UPS, a trend similarly affecting American universities nationally, much as Court indicated for the UK (Court, 1998).

Furthermore, the faculty and students, with assistance from the university staff and several non-CETI corporations in California, ended the CETI arrangement noted above, which would have granted unparalleled control over university activities to outside business firms, including Microsoft. Again, the odds seemed slim for the faculty staff and students to emerge victorious against such formidable opposition. But, at a major legislative hearing on January 6 1998 in Sacramento, huge opposition was registered that became the beginning of the end for CETI. This is further evidence that faculty, students and staff are increasingly aware of the threats to higher education and are increasingly willing to initiate political actions to combat the threats.

5.   Conclusion

There remain battles to be fought over distance learning, especially if introduced without faculty participation and control. Some of the issues still to be resolved include: assessments of student learning outcomes, especially when outcomes are connected to higher education funding; copyright ownership of faculty courses, especially related to the increasing use of distance learning; the increasingly heavy reliance on part-time faculty staff; the support of tenure in the face of severe attacks; the persisting issue of faculty salaries, especially in growth economies where increased money is available for public allocations, but allocations remain uncertain; and university governance, complicated by university administrators collaborating with business firms in attempts to dictate university policies. However, we have seen that the faculty is no longer complacent or compliant and, combined with students and other university staff, can put up organised opposition to encroachments from the administration and outside business interests to retain or regain control of the modern university.

References

American Association of University Professors (1993), 'San Diego State University: An administration's response to fiscal stress', *Academe,* March/April 1993: 94-118.

American Sociological Association (1997), 'San Diego State Creates Legal Defense Fund', ASA *Footnotes,* May/June 1993: 9.

Bernstein, R. (1992), 'The Yale Schmidt Leaves Behind', *The New York Times Magazine*, June 14 1992: 33, 46, 48, 58, 64.

Cook, A. and Kirk G. (1984), *Greenham Women Everywhere*. London: Pluto Press.

Court, S. (1998), 'Academic tenure and employment in the UK' *,Sociological Perspectives.* 41(4): 767-774.

DeGroot, G.J. (ed.) (1998), *Student protest: The Sixties and after.* London and New York: Addison Wesley Longman.

e-mail public announcements from CFA (1999). e-mail messages from the California Faculty Association (CFA) about the collective bargaining contract between CFA and the California State University (CSU) system

e-mail public announcements at SDSU (1997), Several administrative personnel changes announced on San Diego State University's campus-wide e-mail network in the Spring and Summer.

Evans, M. (1999), 'No contract, no participation', *The Daily Aztec.* April 15 1999: 1, 4.

Farber, J. (1998), 'The third circle: On education and distance learning', *Sociological Perspectives,* 41(4): 797-814.

FCPHE (Faculty Coalition for Public Higher Education) (1999), 'Symposium report: Faculty question corporate model for public higher education', *Newsletter*, 3(4).

Finkin, M.W. (ed.). (1996), *The Case for Tenure.* Ithaca, New York: ILR Press, an imprint of Cornell University Press.

Ginsberg, A. (1959), *Howl, and other poems.* San Francisco: City Lights Books.

Hohm, C.F. and Wood, J.L. (eds.) (1998), 'Special Issue on "The Academy Under Siege"', *Sociological Perspectives,* 41(4).

Ingram, R.T. (1999), 'Faculty angst and the search for a common enemy', *The Chronicle of Higher Education*, May 14 1999: B-10.

Kantrowitz, B. and King, P. (1992), 'Failing economics: California built a great higher-ed system. Now it's being dismantled', *Newsweek.* September 28 1992: 32-33.

Leik, R.K. (1998), 'There's far more than tenure on the butcher block: A larger context for the recent crisis at the University of Minnesota', *Sociological Perspectives,* 41(4): 747-755.

Los Angeles Times (1999), 'Cal State trustees approve new faculty contract, raises', June 2 1999.

Magner, D.K. (1997), 'A fierce battle over tenure at the U. of Minnesota comes to a quiet close', *The Chronicle of Higher Education,* June 20 1997: A14.

Marchese, T. (1998), 'Not-so-distant competitors: How new providers are remaking the postsecondary market', *AAHE Bulletin of the American Association of Higher Education.*May 1998.

The National Commission on Excellence in Education (1983), *A Nation at Risk.* Washington, D.C.: The Commission: [Superintendent of Documents, United States Government Printing Office, distributor]

Noble, D.F. (1998a), 'Digital diploma mills: The automation of higher education', *Monthly Review,* 49(9): 38-52.

Noble, D.F. (1998b), 'Digital diploma mills, Part II: The coming battle over online instruction', *Sociological Perspectives,* 41(4): 815-825.

Ristine, J. (1995), 'SDSU's president to quit in '96: Was asked to step down earlier than he planned', *San Diego Union-Tribune,* February 2 1995: A1, A11.

Selingo, J. (1999), 'New chancellor shakes up Cal. State with ambitious agenda and blunt style', *The Chronicle of Higher Education,* June 11 1999.

Snow, C.P. (1959), *The Two Cultures.* Cambridge: Cambridge University Press.

The Chronicle of Higher Education, (1999), 'Academics in Britain have made good on their threat to strike for higher wages', June 4 1999: A49.

Wood, J.L. (1998a.), 'The academy under siege: An outline of problems and strategies', *Sociological Perspectives,* 41(4): 833-847.

Wood, J.L. (1998b), 'With a little help from our friends: Student activism and the crisis at San Diego State University', in: (DeGroot, 1998): 264-279.

Wood, J.L. and Valenzuela L.T. (1996), 'The crisis of American higher education', *Thought and action: The NEA higher education journal*, XII(2): 59-71.

Wood, J.L. and Valenzuela L.T. (1997), 'The crisis in higher education', in: Hohm, C.F. (ed.) (1997), *California's Social Problems.* New York: Longman. 81-98.

Atatvistic Avatars: Ontology, Education and 'Virtual Worlds'

Adrian Bromage

Abstract

This speculative and conceptual chapter considers evidence that synchronous social encounters in multi-user Virtual Reality (VR) systems have an atavistic quality, retaining the essential character of those in 'real life', and explores the likely practical consequences for educators. The discussion begins with an overview of different kinds of VR world, which range from those in which the participants have a second-order perspective to those in which they have a first-order perspective from the point of view of a personalised 'avatar' which is under their control. Ontological questions are then considered. Davis' analysis of 'avatar ontology' is read in terms of existential phenomenology (Davis, 1998). It seems that the 'representative' iconography of avatars can enable participants to 'occupy' a virtual world in an embodied form. This raises the possibility that first-order and face-to-face educational encounters and those in avatar-populated virtual worlds may differ only in degree rather than kind. In exploring this question, analogies are drawn between synchronous learning communities and the virtual reality 'E-Church' studied by Schroeder et al (Schroeder et al, 1998). It seems likely that the essential features of synchronous learning communities, including a genuine feeling of community, can be reproduced in virtual reality, albeit in a less orderly way and with less emotional solidarity between participants and with the emergence of novel behaviours enabled by the technology. Significant questtions are raised for online learning. For example, what are the minimum technological and socio-psychological circumstances in which genuine feelings of community will arise, and with what level of reduced emotional solidarity between participants? It may be possible to manage the less orderly nature of encounters in virtual reality in a way that facilitates students' engagement and peer-supported learning. Some recent findings from the evaluation of Coventry University's campus-wide Learn Online initiative are explored to throw light on these issues.

1. The Nature of Virtual Reality

In considering the issues that this chapter seeks to address, one starting point is to explore the experiences of participants in VR worlds. In such worlds, several participants simultaneously access a database comprising a number of 'rooms'. Each participant controls a personalised 'avatar' that can display text-messages and interact in real-time with both other avatars and the virtual environment. Schroeder differentiates three kinds of VR (Schroeder, 1997): in 'immersive VR', participants wear input/output devices such as head-mounted displays and 'data gloves', and have a first-person perspective on a graphical three-dimensional virtual environment from their avatar's point-of-view; in 'desktop VR', participants have a first-person view from their avatar's perspective displayed on their two-dimensional desktop computer screen; finally, in 'second-person VR' systems, participants are again represented on-screen as an avatar but have a have a second-order view on a two-dimensional environment. It seems that VR enables participants to experience a sense of embodiment in an environment other than the one they physically inhabit (Lee et al, 1997; Schroeder 1997). Schroeder stresses that the combined effect of using text, navigating a virtual environment and engaging with other users via avatars is greater than the sum of its parts; even second-person VR generates a feeling of immersion in a virtual environment.

Descriptions and screenshot images of a number of virtual worlds and related technical information can be found in the literature (Lee et al, 1997; Schroeder 1997). The visual style of virtual worlds ranges anywhere between something comprising descriptions of 'rooms' in plain text only and where participants communicate using plain text to very realistic-looking worlds that are populated by avatars which take the form of fairly realistic-looking human figures. (Those who wish to try 'desktop VR' can access Activeworld's 'Alpha World' at the following URL: http://www.activeworlds.com/).

2.   The Educational Use of Virtual Reality

Educationalists have recently begun to explore the academic potential of computer-generated VR systems (Lee et al, 1997). The use of VR in an educational context tends either explicitly or implicitly to have at its heart a philosophy of social constructivism. Bird argues that the philosophy places community, dialogue and shared understanding centre-stage (Bird, 2002). An example from the US schools sector is ExploreNet, which has been used to help learners to develop the skills necessary to construct virtual worlds for peer-supported learning of particular concepts (Hughes and Moshell, 1995; Schroeder, 1997). Participants' avatars are allocated different roles and capabilities in terms of their interaction with the world and others' avatars. Teachers and adult volunteers facilitate the learning process which is explicitly based upon constructivist principles.

Another example, of some technical interest, is LinguaMoo from the US higher education sector (Holmevik and Haynes, 2000). This is primarily intended as a space where students can meet as a community and collaborate on research projects. The software application runs on HTML browsers which makes it highly accessible. Its specification supports a 'second-person VR'. Each participant has their presence denoted by a static avatar which is visually little more than a head and shoulders in silhouette. Avatars have a limited capacity for limited interaction with a virtual environment that comprises a number of 'rooms'. Each room consists of static 2-D images that function as if they were 'backdrops' to the scene. Below the backdrops are hyperlinks to other rooms and icons that represent the objects and the other avatars who occupy the room.

A more recently developed example, from the UK schools sector, is Edrama, a Nesta-funded project created by Hi8us Projects Ltd (Midlands). Edrama is currently being piloted at Queensbridge School, a non-selective state school situated around three miles from Birmingham city centre whose student are boys and girls of diverse cultural backgrounds who are aged between eleven and sixteen (Kenny 2002). Edrama uses immersive techniques such as improvisation to encourage students to respond to and learn from different scenarios in a safe and controlled environment. The participants each anonymously role-play a particular character whose avatar they control. Together they improvise through a pre-determined scenario in real-time under the supervision of a Director, typically a teacher. Kenny quotes one teacher at the school who reports that during a typical session the participants sit in silence in front of their computer terminals, typing furiously and concentrating intently upon the events that are unfolding rapidly on-screen. Both teacher and pupil comment positively on the socially levelling and liberating effects of their anonymity and the freedom created to explore different personae to their usual ones. Given the social constructivist model at the heart of many of the educational applications of VR, the key issues for educationalists are arguably how and to what extent electronic environments can support a sense of community and dialogue. In exploring these issues it is useful to consider ontological questions.

3.   The Ontology of Virtual Reality

The feeling of immersion within VR that participants experience phenomenally implies that a Cartesian ontological perspective, with its subject-object dichotomy, would be inadequate as a framework with which to understand how this can be so. Indeed, an emerging radical anti-Cartesian ontological perspective on the phenomenon of VR is held by those whom Sullins refers to as 'Transhumanists' (Sullins, 2000). Rushkoff describes the philosophies and beliefs of 'Cyberian countercultures' of the USA which are arguably representative of the Transhumanist position (Rushkoff, 1994). They view the Internet as enabling us to access cyberspace, a 'dimensional plane' where time, space and the body are transcended and we can create our own realities merely by thinking them. Participating in VR can help the 'Cyberians' to recognise aspects of our world that are arbitrary and temporary, helping in their endeavours to free themselves of such arbitrary constraints. Furthermore, the Cyberians hold the controversial belief that the multidimensional and highly interconnected nature of reality means that changing one's construal of it changes its very physical matter. It will be seen that this belief has implications for their view of the human in cyberspace.

Rushkoff discusses the Cyberians' notion that one's consciousness temporarily transcends the physical body and enters cyberspace generated within a computer network, and when this occurs it might be capable of permanently transferring itself into cyberspace. It is arguable that the other techniques that Rushkoff describes by which cyberspace can be accessed, for example pagan ritual, dance, and psychoactive drugs, involve the generation of an altered state of consciousness. Insofar as they interact with it to produce the effect, the techniques depend to some extent upon the body and its perceptual apparatus. This could also be said of the human-computer interface. Indeed, Sullins criticises the Transhumanist agenda on ontological grounds, arguing that the 'transcendent mind hypothesis', which holds that immersive VR enables the mind to transcend the body, is flawed since it fails to address the embodied nature of those who participate in immersive VR. Sullins makes reference to the philosophy of Maurice Merleau-Ponty in his arguments, and this is worthy of closer consideration.

Merleau-Ponty originally formulated the philosophy of existential phenomenology, which, it will be seen, has recently been developed by Varela (Varela, 1994). Its central notion is that human existence both unifies and transcends consciousness and the world. Spurling regards Heidegger and Sartre, both of whom conceived phenomenology as the study of the intertwining of 'facts' (the phenomenal) and 'essences' (the properties of the world) in how the world forms around us, as the existential influences on Merleau-Ponty (Spurling, 1977). Merleau-Ponty's philosophy is existentialist to the extent that its study of knowledge and thought is grounded on a concrete analysis of existence that emphasises action. Spurling argues that to these ends Merleau-Ponty reworked Husserl's notion of 'intentionality', the relationship between consciousness and the world, into 'operative intentionality', a unity in which the world is a 'signifying' pole and consciousness an 'expressive' pole that enables us to experience our environment as a meaningful unity, our life-world or reality. (A detailed discussion of the intellectual history of Merleau-Ponty's philosophy has been undertaken by Schmidt (Schmidt, 1985)). Existential phenomenology holds that our beliefs and desires act to condition our perceptions of the world and, by extension, our subsequent actions. The implication is that changing one's beliefs can ultimately change one's world. However, this is somewhat different to the 'Transhumanist' position regarding the effects of beliefs on physical matter as it refers to perception of and action in the world.

A discernibly existentialist stance is evident in many recent books and papers that analyse the relationship between humans and technology. Pepperell suggests that human beings are intertwined as one with the technology that surrounds them and calls this the 'Post-Human' condition (Pepperell, 1995). However, existential phenomenology suggests that this may be both something of a misnomer and nothing new, merely another manifestation of the 'intentional arc' in action. In a similar vein McAlees views the process of educational innovation as a praxis integrating both theory and artefact into programmes that can be characterised as a 'technology of education', as an interplay of the theories of education that serve as intellectual frameworks and the tools deployed, as 'technology in education' (McAlees, 1997). The central question, it seems, is the extent to which our interaction with virtual environments takes us into a new realm of being-in-the-world as opposed to it being a particularly sophisticated example of tool use.

Davis takes a discernibly existentialist stance in his analysis of our interaction with communication and information technologies (C&IT) (Davis, 1998). He sees computers and their users as a techno-cultural hybrid in which computers "create a new interface between the self, the other and the world beyond" and as such are part of all three. He argues that like other communication media, C&IT transcend their status as 'things' by supporting the "incorporeal transmission of mind and meaning". Davis coins the phrase 'Avatar Ontology' to refer to our 'being-with-computers' and proposes that when one surfs the Internet one becomes a 'homocyber'. Nelson-Kilger presses this general point further, arguing that 'virtual selves' capable of exchanging meaningful symbols during interactions with other 'virtual' and 'physical' selves are true members of the social world, and that this opens up the possibility of a parallel 'digital society' (Nelson-Kilger, 1993).

Davis argues that C&IT cannot be viewed as a neutral tool through which an assumed immutable human nature can be extended. He cautions that throughout history, the invention of significant new communication devices has led not only to new opportunities but also to unintended consequences that are new traps for thought, perception and social experience. Indeed, Nelson-Kilger argues that the possibility of a parallel 'digital society' may have serious consequences for our privacy and freedom.

If read in terms of existential phenomenology, the arguments above are suggestive of ontological grounds for our embodiment as social beings within VR. The philosophy holds that the source of our experience of 'reality' is neither an independent physical world nor consciousness alone, but rather their intercourse in a unified world-body-consciousness system that is conceptualised as 'being-in-the-world'. The underlying mechanism is 'operative intentionality', a pre-reflective 'dialogue' between the 'signifying' world and our 'expressive' consciousness which projects around us an 'intentional arc' that we experience as our reality. For example, an object's colour is 'intentional', a signifying property aimed

outside of those purely physical properties giving rise to it that is expressed
as a sensation within those beings having the appropriate perceptual
apparatus.

This may help to explain why participants in VR can feel as they
are immersed within. Computers render the electronic environment
perceivable and thus capable of acting as a 'signifying pole' within the
dialectic of 'operative intentionality'. In this reading, VR is arguably not a
'hyperreal' in the sense proposed by Baudrillard, "the generation by
models of a real without origin or reality" (Baudrillard, 1983, 2). It also
carries the implication that the term 'virtual reality', defined in the Collins
English Dictionary as "a computer-generated environment that, to the
person experiencing it, closely resembles reality" may be something of a
misnomer (Grandison et al, 1994: 1714). There is a sense in which it is a
genuine, albeit 'synthetic' reality.

Both Davis' and Nelson-Kilger's arguments can be read in terms
of Varela's development of the 'linguistic turn' within the philosophy, a
move which raises questions regarding the relationship between
participants' sense of embodiment within and social interactions in VR
environments (Varela, 1994). Varela suggests that in his later works,
Merleau-Ponty took a 'linguistic turn' and moved towards viewing 'being'
as primarily cultural, lived socially and experienced psychologically. To
these ends he revises Harre's conversational realism to refer to the
"enactment of gestural systems of non-vocal and vocal semiotic acts"
(Harre, 1983. Varela argues that utterances as causal powers are
inseparable from substance and agency, all three coming together in
'personhood', which is conceived as capable of causally empowered
agency.

What might constitute 'gesture' within electronic environments?
Schroeder argues that users of communication technologies must transmit
'social cues' through whatever 'communication channels' the technology
affords (Schroeder, 1997). Nelson-Kilger sees the key issue as one of
'bandwidth' (Nelson-Kilger, 1993). Face-to-face interactions have
tremendous bandwidth; to convey and read both verbal and, importantly,
non-verbal communication cues we engage all of our senses (including
taste if one considers potential of the shared experience of eating in this
respect.). In contrast, digital technologies can severely limit the bandwidth
of available communication channels; for example, in synchronous text-
only Computer-Mediated Communication (CMC), we are to all intents and
purposes limited to vision. Even synchronous video conferencing has a
limited bandwidth in comparison to face-to-face encounters; for example,
the subtle touching that is often an important part of everyday
communication is absent and in cyberspace no one can smell your
expensive perfume.

Nelson-Kilger argues that one response of text-only CMC users has been the development of 'emoticons', which are limited to conveying primarily affective behaviours such as happiness or sadness, the infamous 'smiley' being a good example. Another strategy is to deploy multiple information sources; for example, exchanges of status information and so on between correspondents. This is not necessarily a straightforward process. Based on the finding that creators of Web-pages are less accurate at judging the nature of the impressions of themselves that they convey to others online than in face-to-face situations, Sherman et al argue that the challenge facing those who seek to manage their online personae is to take account of bandwidth limitations (Sherman et al, 2001). However, despite the potential pitfalls, Asenio et al found evidence that participants in text-only discussion forums pay a great deal of attention to how they express their meanings and emotions, and they argue that this tends to support Derrida's argument that writing is a vehicle through which rich and considered views of the world can be conveyed (Asenio et al, 2000; Derrida, 1967).

Synchronous text-based CMC has more bandwidth than asynchronous CMC because it introduces co-presence. Virtual worlds populated by avatars have still greater bandwidth. It is arguable that the 'representative' iconography of avatars introduces an implicit spatial metaphor. The avatar acts to personalise messages, the window of the text message becoming at some level an iconographic 'mouth'. Furthermore, it maintains a visible presence when not engaged in textual communication that might convey at least something of an individual's 'style' of being-in-the-world, by its location in various areas of a virtual world for example. Avatars enable participants not only to 'occupy' the virtual world, but to act upon it. In LinguaMoo for example, the participants can gag another's avatar or lock the door of the room they currently occupy by typing special commands on the keyboard.

Schroeder compares text-based CMC and multi-user VR (Schroeder, 1997). On the basis of the notion that the sociological significance of new technologies lies in how they intensify or extend novel opportunities and constraints for manipulating the natural and social worlds, he argues that the significance of multi-user VR may lie in how it extends the novel features of text-based CMC technologies. For example, exploring different milieus in imaginary text-based rooms becomes exploring landscapes and rooms. Sustaining relationships, which is achieved in text-based CMC with entertaining banter, now requires that participants 'do' things together. The sense of belonging to an established group that is created through text-based exchanges becomes a sense of belonging created through physical proximity. Turned upside-down, Schroeder's arguments imply that text-based CMC supports the maintenance of social relationships, joint exploration of different milieus and the existence of social groups. Indeed, Curtis concludes in relation to text-based VR that these features are essentially throwbacks to face-to-face social behaviours (Curtis, 1992).

That the participants in electronic environments can experience a sense of belonging raises the issue of their attachment to the electronic environment. Notable in Schroeder's examples is a 'spatial' metaphor which opens up interesting possibilities in this respect. Twigger-Ross and Uzzell sought to explore the relationship between personal identity and the physical environment. They hypothesised that those who have a sense of attachment to their locale have consider it in terms of the four principles of personal identity identified by Breakwell in his 'identity process' model (Breakwell, 1986; Breakwell, 1992; Breakwell, 1993; Twigger-Ross and Uzzell, 1996). These are: distinctiveness of individual identity; continuity with the past; self-esteem; and self-efficacy (which Wood and Bandura conceptualise as ones' perceived competence to act in a manner that meets the demands of a given situation) (Wood and Bandura, 1989). Breakwell's conceptualisation of identity is discernibly existential in its orientation since it is in terms of a biological organism that moves through time and whose development proceeds through accommodating, assimilating and evaluating its social environment (Breakwell, 1986). Twigger-Ross and Uzzell found that there is a clear relationship between an individual's identity and their attachment to their locale in terms of these four principles (Twigger-Ross and Uzzell, 1996). It would certainly seem that there is scope to deploy this approach to the analysis of the individual's attachment to electronic environments, and in particular first-person VR worlds. The implication is that the way we act within such environments has an atavistic quality in that it reflects the way we occupy the 'physical' world.

4.   The Possibility of an E-University

The implications of the above arguments for the comparability between synchronous educational encounters in multi-user VR systems and those in the physical world will now be considered. The relatively large 'bandwidth' of avatar-populated virtual worlds opens the possibility that they may differ in degree rather than kind. In considering this issue, analogies are drawn between the university as a learning community and the virtual-reality E-Church that was the subject of Schroeder et al's non-participant observation (Schroeder et al, 1998). Christian churches arguably have an educational function. They seek to impart a particular world-view and enable worshippers to internalise it using a technique, akin to lectures by acknowledged experts, of a minister addressing a congregation, reinforced with pastoral one-to-one support. Participants, represented by animated avatars, convene at a set time in a particular place for a particular experience, as do students attending university lectures or seminars.

Schroeder et al found that social interactions within the E-Church tend to be more structured than in other virtual worlds. Services take place at fixed weekly times in a fixed locale with several regular participants. Schroeder et al also compare services in the E-Church to those in a physical church. There is evidence of an open, informal and interactive 'charismatic' style. Certain behaviours borrow from other technologies - for example, the use of 'emoticons' from text-based CMC and playful behaviours after services akin to those in computer games such as 'flying' or going through walls. The technology does not, however, completely reshape social relations. There is a sense in which participants feel co-present to co-ordinate their 'voices' and focus their collective attention on the object of their worship such that group cohesion is reinforced.

There are advantages and disadvantages to this. The technology facilitates candid exchanges, enables international access and permits experiments in design and use of a virtual space that are less constrained than in a conventional church. However, some social practices are transformed in ways that perhaps detract from a sense of religious gathering. Verbal exchanges tend to be shorter, 'worshippers' have weaker emotional solidarity and prayer meetings are less orderly. As in other forms of CMC, participants may 'disguise' their identities, making the sincerity of confessions or promises of betterment seem less credible than those made face-to-face. Despite these caveats, Schroeder et al conclude that while E-Church prayer meetings may not provide the same religious experience as conventional church services, some of the essential features are reproduced, albeit in novel ways, and thus the E-Church perpetuates the role of the sacred in society.

Schroeder et al's findings have significant implications for online learning, particularly for the possibilities of a 'virtual reality e-university'. It is arguable that the essential features of educational encounters in a university can be reproduced in a virtual world, albeit transformed, such that they would be less orderly and feature whatever novel behaviours are enabled by the technology. Importantly, although it might be expected that there will be less emotional solidarity between participants it seems possible that genuine feelings of community might emerge. It is interesting at this point to refer back to earlier discussion of the ontology of VR. The picture that Schroeder et al's findings paint of a VR environment suggest that it would present participants with plenty of food for thought in terms of recognising those aspects of their world that are arbitrary. The latter represents a vein that certainly has the potential to be exploited by educationalists working in fields such as philosophy or the social sciences.

5.   The Comparability of 'Face-to-Face' and 'Virtual' Education
At present the possibilities outlined above represent mere speculation. UK universities have tended to deploy online learning

experiences within the context of their existing face-to-face provision. For example, Coventry University's institution-wide Learn Online initiative seeks to support face-to-face andragogic activities with the online 'virtual learning' environment (VLE) WebCT, based on, in Mason's term, a 'wrap-around' model (Mason, 1999). WebCT in many ways replicates the classroom in an online environment. For example, it has facilities for delivering lesson content and conducting on-line assessment although there are also facilities for synchronous and asynchronous text-only CMC discussions. It is perhaps worth contrasting WebCT with Colloquia, a 'portable' VLE that realises a conversationally-based group-learning model (Liber 2000). However, this raises questions concerning what minimum technological and socio-psychological circumstances might be necessary for genuine group cohesion to arise and with what level of reduction in emotional solidarity between participants.

To address these questions it is useful to begin by considering the general relationship between the social world and its technological artefacts. In his comparison of multi-user VR and text-based CMC technologies, Schroeder argues that the sociological importance of new technologies lies in the novel opportunities and constraints they afford for refining and manipulating the natural and social worlds (Schroeder, 1997). Schroeder concludes that multi-user VR might essentially extend the novel features of text-based CMC environments which it has been seen are themselves capable of sustaining the feeling of a community of participants.

Recent findings from research into Coventry University's campus-wide Learn Online initiative will now be explored in relation to some of the issues above. There is some evidence that academic discussions in text-based CMC can strengthen feelings of an academic community for groups of students who pursue the same course of study. Bell has exploited the WebCT Discussion Forum to support small group work within a cohort of 180 first-year students, with the intention that relatively small groups combined with WebCT's privacy would create a reassuring and liberating climate (Bell, 2002b). Indeed, Bell found that the approach helped to foster mutual support and respect between students, their peers and the course tutor. Orsini-Jones deployed the Discussion Forum and Chat facilities of WebCT in a collaborative approach to group work based on an underlying constructivist philosophy (Orsini-Jones, 2002a). She found that this approach helped to increase cohesion within what was a diverse group of students and to encourage peer support and 'democratic' relations with tutors.

In relation to students' social engagement, several unintended, though welcome, consequences of using WebCT have emerged. Orsini-Jones found evidence that shier students contribute more to online than face-to-face discussions because they can plan their discourse (Orsini-

Jones, 2002b). Similarly, Brooke and Jenkins found some evidence that those for whom English is a second language find it easier to participate in asynchronous CMC discussions. Perhaps the most interesting consequence is reported by Bell (2002a), who found that posting lecture notes on WebCT for students to discuss with both their peers and the lecturers themselves led to an increase in the number of students attending each lecture. Bell suspects they are attracted by the face-to-face 'lecture experience', which is qualitatively different to reading notes on a computer screen, especially since posting notes on WebCT frees the tutor to concentrate on making the experience memorable.

The question of trust seems to enter the picture. Although Orsini-Jones does not explicitly address this issue, it is implicit in her finding that the discussion facilities of WebCT have a 'democratising' effect upon student-tutor relations (Orsini-Jones, 2002a). However, it seems that this is a consequence of the way in which the participants' use of text-based CMC is structured rather than something that springs automatically from its use. Orsini-Jones' students were largely campus-based, and so would at least 'see each other around', if not actually engage in social chat. Rocco found that when participants who have never met negotiate by email, the levels of trust generated between participants are lower than in face-to-face negotiation (Rocco, 1998). However, when participants completed a face-to-face team-building exercise prior to engaging in email negotiations, Rocco found that the levels of trust generated in the email condition were similar to those in the face-to-face condition. In a later study, Zheng et al found that engaging participants in a brief period of face-to-face social chat prior to email was sufficient to raise levels of trust such that there was no difference to the level of trust reported in face-to-face negotiations (Zheng et al, 2001).

Regarding the question of the intellectual quality of students' work in online environments, Brooke and Jenkins explore the claim made on behalf of WebCT that the asynchronous Discussion Forum facility can replicate the conditions of a face-to-face seminar (Brooke and Jenkins, 2000). The tutors in their case study sought to make the WebCT Discussion Forum as user-friendly as a commercial Internet chat site. Brooke and Jenkins deploy discourse analysis that takes as its benchmark what is arguably the andragogic technique of 'elite' Higher Education, Socratic dialogue in which a tutor questions learners about some topic in order that they jointly explore and develop their understanding. Brooke and Jenkins conclude that the medium, or perhaps specifically this particular model for its use, does not support sustained high-quality academic debate. The electronic discourse that the authors made the subject of their analysis was judged to have the linguistic characteristics of 'casual conversation', inhibiting academic content by dispersing it among 'allusive wisecracks'. These conclusions contrast with Bell's findings in relation to his use of the

WebCT Discussion Forum to support small group discussions with a large cohort of first-year students on a Typography module (Bell, 2002b). Bell found the academic standard of students' discussions to be very high, exhibiting great sophistication for students at this level.

The issue of the alignment between CMC and two educational stances will now be considered. Brooke and Jenkins argue that the asynchronicity of the text-only WebCT Discussion Forum disrupts the delicate balance of interactions between participants (Brooke and Jenkins, 2000). In consequence the thread of consecutive ideas, necessary for academic debate modelled on Socratic dialogue, becomes merely associative. In contrast, Bird argues that text-only CMC can support action learning (Bird, 2002). Bird identifies social constructivism as the underlying philosophy of this approach and argues that the loss of co-presence between participants is relatively unimportant given that constructivist philosophy views language as both a form of action and the vehicle for reality construction. Bird argues on this basis that the central issue is not co-presence but students' meaningful engagement through interaction with others on common tasks that is perceived to be worthwhile.

There is some evidence to support Bird's assertion. Bell found that online discussions where students must engage with others on specific tasks yield high-quality debate (Bell, 2002a); Bell, 2002b). Indeed Brooke and Jenkins' finding that students perceive online discussions modelled on commercial chat-sites as "somewhere between the pleasantries of gossip and the intellectual stimulation of a well-focused seminar" is suggestive that one weakness of this particular approach was that it failed to foster intellectual engagement within the participating students (Brooke and Jenkins, 2000).

6.   Conclusions

In summary, there exists evidence to suggest that a sense of community can be fostered where education takes place within virtual learning environments if their use is carefully structured and takes account of the atavistic quality of social relations between participants in VR. It seems that the central issue for those who would establish such communities, whether in text-based CMC or Virtual Worlds, is to ensure that the participants engage socially with one another when meaningfully involved on common course-related activities that are perceived to be worthwhile. Even so, it should be anticipated that the technologies which support the virtual learning environment will to some extent transform the nature of the educational encounter. In particular, it is likely that there will be an underlying tension between the tutors' need to structure their students' use of the environment and the likelihood that social relations within the VLE will tend to be less orderly than those in first-person face-to-face settings. This may be offset by the very real possibility that the transformation will bring unanticipated benefits such as increased levels of participation from certain groups of students who would tend to become marginalised in face-to-face education.

More surprisingly, it seems that the large-group face-to-face lecture format can be invigorated if it is integrated carefully with online content delivery and discussions. This may become an important consideration given that many students value the opportunity for face-to-face social interaction with their tutors and for immersion in the general milieu of university life. This is particularly so for those from overseas who study in the UK (Selwyn, 2000). However, Zheng et al's conclusions suggest that a face-to-face social meeting prior to the start of a course may at least be enough to generate trust between participants in VR (Zheng et al, 2001). Furthermore Chih-Hsiung's exploration of Chinese students' perceptions of CMC highlights the importance of taking account of the interaction between international students' culturally-preferred communication styles, their level of technical skills and the nature of electronic learning environments (Chih-Hsiung, 2001).

One particular caveat that relates to the educational use of VLE's has not been addressed in the studies cited above. Lievrouw argues that in virtual social contexts, a distinctive style of communication has emerged (Lievrouw, 1998). This is 'heterotopic communication', whereby individuals appear to be open and cooperative by virtue of their use of information and communication technologies, yet actively avoid exposure to anything that challenges their purposes or world-views. Lievrouw argues that this mode of communication rests in part upon ideology, in the form of a prevailing western ethic of self-interest, and a belief that communication technologies are socially-integrative. However, Lievrouw cautions that heterotopic communication may lead to social separatism and parochialism and may be socially divisive. The implication is that an e-university, or even a conventional university within which VLE's are widely used, may be in greater danger of fragmentation than those institutions making minimal use of such environments unless care is taken to ensure that the staff and students have meaningful opportunities to communicate beyond their own individual courses and disciplines.

To end on a purely speculative note, one potential strand of inquiry into the issue of how a sense of community might be developed that is not explored in the studies cited above is the relationship between individual students' developing identity and their participation in online environments during their studies. It might be an interesting exercise to deploy the methodology developed by Twigger-Ross and Uzzell to these ends (Twigger-Ross and Uzzell, 1996).

References

Asenio, M., Hodgeson, V., and Trehan, K. (2000), 'Is there a difference?: Contrasting experiences of face to face and online learning', in: Asenio, M., Hodgeson, V., Foster, J. and McConnell, D. (2000) (eds.) *Proceedings of the 2nd International Conference, networked learning*.12-19.

Baudrillaurd, J. (1983), *Simulations*. (trans. Foss, P. et al.), New York: Semiotext(e).

Bell, S. (2002a), *Talking pictures on the web*. http://home.edu.coventry.ac.uk/webctwise/121GD/121gd_ov.htm (accessed 16 July 2003).

Bell, S. (2002b), *What did he just say?... better check his WebCT notes!* Available   from http://home.edu.coventry.ac.uk/webctwise/SimonB/SB_lectures.htm (accessed 16 July 2003).

Bird, L. (2002), 'Action Learning sets: the case for running them online', in: Banks, S., Goodyear, P., Hodegson, V. and McConnell, D. (eds.) (2002), *Networked Learning 2002*. Sheffield: Lancaster University and University of Sheffield.

Breakwell, G.M. (1986), *Coping with threatened identity*. London: Methuen.

Breakwell, G.M. (1992), 'Processes of self-evaluation: Efficacy and estrangement', in: Breakwell, G.M. (ed.) *Social Psychology of Identity*. Surrey: Surrey University Press.

Breakwell, G. M. (1993), 'Integrating paradigms: Methodological implications', in: G. M. Breakwell and D. V. Cantor (eds.) *Empirical Approaches to Social Representation*. Oxford: Clarendon Press.

Brooke, B. and Jenkins, D. (2000), *The analysis of bulleting board traffic: two case studies*. Coventry: Coventry University Centre for Higher Education   Development. http://www.ched.coventry.ac.uk/ched/Research/bulbbdj.htm (accessed 16 July 2003).

Chih-Hsiung, T. (2001), 'How Chinese perceive social presence: An examination of interaction in online learning environment." *Educational Media International,* 38(1): 45-46.
Curtis, P. (1992), 'Mudding: Social phenomena in text-based virtual realities', *Proceedings of the 1992 conference on the directions and implications of advanced computing.* http://citeseer.nj.nec.com/curtis92mudding.html (accessed 8 July 2003).

Davis, E. (1998), *Techgnosis: Myth, magic and mysticism in the age of information.* New York: Harmony Books.

Derrida, J. (1967), *De La Grammatology.* Paris: Minuit. (Trans) Chakravoty-Spivak, G. *Of Grammatology.* The John Hopkins University Press, 1967.

Grandison, A., McGinley, D., Shearer, T., Knight, L., Summers, E., Lyons, C. and Forde, C. (eds.) (1994), *Collins English Dictionary* (3rd. Ed.) London: HarperCollins.

Harre, R. (1983), *Personal Being.* Oxford: Blackwell.

Holmevik, J.R. and Haynes, C. (2000), *Linguamoo.* Available at http://www.dartmouth.edu/~webteach/cases/linguamoo.html (Accessed 8 July 2003)

Hughes, C., and Moshell, M. (1995), *Shared virtual worlds for education: The ExploreNet experiment.* http://www.cs.ucf.edu/~ExploreNet/papers/VA.Experiment1195.html (accessed 1 January 2003).

Kenny, J. (2002), 'You're online, be yourself', *The Guardian Education,* June 11 2002: 8.

Lee, S., Groves, P., Stephens, C. and Armitage, S. (1997), *Guide to online teaching: Existing tools and projects.* Joint Information Systems Committee (JISC) Technology Applications Project, 1997. http://www.jtap.ac.uk/reports/htm/jtap-028.htm#forward (accessed 1 January 2003).

Liber, O. (2000), 'Colloquia - a conversation manager', *Campus-Wide Information Systems,* 17(2).
Lievrouw, L.A. (1998), 'Our own devices: Heterotopic communication, discourse, and culture in the information society', *The Information Society,* 14(2): 83-96.

McAlees, R. (1997), 'Technology in education to technology of education: Concepts, conflicts and compromises', in: S. Armstrong, G. Thompson, and S. Brown (eds) *Facing up to radical changes in universities and colleges.* London: Kogan Page.

Mason, R. (1998), 'Models of online courses', *ALN Magazine,* 2(2). http://www.sloanc.org/publications/magazine/v2n2/mason.asp (accessed 16 July 2003).

Nelson-Kilger, M. (1993), 'The Digital Individual', *The Third Conference on Computers Freedom and Privacy,* March 9-12, 1993, Burlingame, CA. http://www.cpsr.org/conferences/cfp93/nelson-kilger.html (accessed 16 July 2003).

Orsini-Jones, M. (2002a), *A 'meta-use' of WebCT to teach IT for language learning.* http://home.edu.coventry.ac.uk/webctwise/120LAN/120lan_ov.htm (accessed 16 July 2003).

Orsini-Jones, M. (2002b), *Student-Centred Learning in Italian.* http://home.edu.coventry.ac.uk/webctwise/304lai/304lai_ov.htm (accessed 16 July 2003).

Pepperell, R. (1995), *The Post-Human Condition.* Exeter: Intellect Books.

Rocco, E. (1996), 'Trust breaks down in electronic contexts, but can be repaired by some initial face-to-face contact', *Conference proceeedings on Human Factors in Computing Systems.* 496-502.

Rushkoff, D. (1994), *Cyberia: Life in the trenches of hyperspace.* San Fransisco: Harper Collins.

Schroeder, R. (1997), 'Networked worlds: Social aspects of multi-user virtual reality technology', *Sociological Research Online.* 2(4) http://www.socresonline.org.uk/socresonline/2/4/5.html (accessed 1 January 2003).

Schroeder, R., Heather, N. and Lee, R.L. (1998), 'The sacred and the virtual: Religion in multi-user virtual reality', *Journal of computer-mediated communication.* 4(2) http://www.ascusc.org/jcmc/vol4/issue2/schroeder.html (accessed 16 July 2003).

Schmidt, J. (1985), *Maurice Merleau-Ponty: Between phenomenology and structuralism.* London: Macmillan.

Selwyn, N. (2000), 'Net gains or net pains? Business students' use of the Internet', *Higher Education Quarterly.* 54(2): 166-186.

Sherman, R., End, C., Kraan, E., Cole, A., Campbel, J., Klausner, J. and Birchmeier, Z. (2001), 'Metaperception in Cyberspace', *CyberPsychology and behaviour.* 4(1): 123-129.

Spurling, L. (1977), *Phenomenology and the social world: the philosophy of Merleau-Ponty and its relation to the social sciences.* London: Routledge and Kegan Paul.

Sullins, J. (2000), 'Transcending the meat: Immersive technologies and computer mediated bodies', *Journal of experimental and theoretical artificial intelligence.* 12(1): 13-22.

Twigger-Ross, C.L. and Uzzell, D.L. (1996), 'Place and identity processes', *Journal of environmental psychology.* 16(3): 205-220.

Varela, C.R. (1994), 'Harre and Merleau-Ponty: beyond the absent moving body in embodied social theory', *Journal for the theory of social behaviour.* 24(2): 167-185.

Wood, R.E. and Bandura, A. (1989), 'Impact of conceptions of ability on self-regulatory mechanisms and complex decision making', *Journal of personality and social psychology.* 56: 407-415.

Zheng, J., Bos, N.D., Olson, J.S. and Olson, G.M. (2001), 'Trust without touch: Jump-start trust with social chat', in: *Proceedings of CHI 2001, Short papers.* New York: ACM Press.7

Virtual Values: The University in E-Crisis

David Seth Preston

"The philosopher is not a citizen of any community of
ideas. That is what makes him into a philosopher."
Ludwig Wittgenstein (Wittgenstein, 1963)

Abstract
Since the Industrial Revolution, technology has expanded its
influence to impact upon more and more of the world. At work or play the
human being is increasingly faced with technological interfaces. These
technologies often change both our activities and our ambitions (Preston,
2001).
The university has tried various approaches to the challenge of
technology. Whereas Oxbridge tried to ignore it for over a hundred years,
others have greeted technology with open arms. Information and
Communication technologies (ICT) increasingly dominate university
concerns for the future. Today, terms such as 'e-learning' and 'virtual
university' are often voiced with enthusiasm for the 'new age'. Yet
somehow the nagging doubts remain. Is technology a threat to the
university and if so, what form (if any) will the new university take?
This chapter considers whether modern ICT is actually capable of
fulfilling many of the claims of revolutionary impact on the university. It
additionally examines the values that often accompany the technocratic
vision and explores what new forms of university might be more desirable
than one dominated by technocratic values.

1.   The 'Fuzzy' Computer Age
A series of new dawns for a world ideologically revolutionised by
technology have been heralded at regular intervals in the past, often
predicated upon, with hindsight, the most unlikely devices. For example,
Langdon Winner showed how electricity was vociferously forecast to
transform all work into leisure time, as was tomato fertiliser predicted to
end all famine (Winner, 1992). Of course, the failures of previous
predictions does not necessarily negate contemporary forecasts for the
future but they should perhaps render such visions subject to more detailed
examination.
Many writers, such as Daniel Bell, Zbigniew Brzezinski and
Alvin Toffler have claimed that societal rupture is occurring or imminent
as a result of modern technologies, notably electronic communications and
the computer (Bell, 1962; Brzezinski, 1976; Toffler, 1980). Piore and
Sabel have even termed this supposedly imminent event 'the second
industrial divide' (Piore and Sabel, 1984). Robert Pepperell suggests that

computer-related technologies are actually changing the meaning of words like 'human' into definitions that reflect the existing complex interrelationship between ourselves and the technologies around us (Pepperell, 1995). More mundanely, the popular culture reflects a sense that a technologically-based quantum leap in our ideological framework is about to beset us. For example, both Stanley Kubrick's film *2001* and Amitav Gosht's novel *The Calcutta Chromosome* depicts a life-world that is both recognisable and disturbing. Both implicitly suggest that we are about to have our understanding of what computers do completely undermined. Whilst the literary world tends to emphasise the potential threats, to privacy for example, that a computer-age society would bring, others portray the impending rupture as a positive development (Orwell, 1998; Moor, 1990). Indeed Nicolas Negroponte suggests that the computer age will produce an ideological realignment of unprecedented liberty and freedom (Negroponte, 1996). There seems to be a prevailing opinion that the computer age is about to arrive although naturally, given such impending upheaval, little agreement as to what it might look like.

What actually lies behind the computer age vision? Certainly there is little in current technological devices to support it. Even the latest artificial intelligence (AI) devices are extremely unsophisticated in comparison with human capabilities. The former is capable of replicating (or even improving upon) human performance in some of the many tasks performed by the latter. However, it is always the case that a particular AI device has to be built for each of these tasks whilst a single brain is happy to switch between many. In addition, the tasks have to be of a very particular kind to be suitable for AI implementation. More generally, information and communication technologies have remarkable performance only when the space in which they operate complies with a readily defined (if complex) set of rules such as apply in chess or e-procurement systems that make algorithmic decisions based on stock levels. Once computers leave this well-defined space they generally appear extremely (in human terms) one-dimensional. Those who suggest that contemporary modern technology makes transparent the inevitability of an ideological rupture simply cannot have observed the technology at close hand.

My belief is that the source of the posited imminent ideological rupture is the exponential growth of computer technology. For over half a century computer related technology has doubled in performance roughly every 15 months. This is unprecedented for any man-made product. The computer age vision argument runs that as products alter so will humans. The development of the human race is thus reduced to following a technology that that it created itself. Such a vision then amounts to an enormous supposition and a frightening one at that.

The market is a system that legitimates the accumulative ends of a small elite class. The rich get vastly richer ever more quickly, a process Luttwak terms 'turbo-capitalism' (Luttwak, 1998). The professional class is rewarded, provided they are in the correct business, to efficiently deliver these ends. Increasingly however, technology is threatening their rewards with many professions showing depreciating real earnings over the last decade. The worker class has no opportunities for success measured in these terms.

Jurgen Habermas believes the contemporary world is firmly bound to a model of technocratic values (Habermas, 1971). He suggests that technology is not value-free but is tied to the history and culture of the place that it resides in. In particular, the values of technology are highly reflective of ruling interests. What those with the most powerful voices wish to do with technology is what is generally done. Habermas is certainly supported by a good deal of evidence in the modern world. For example the largest research and development spend on computer technology, despite the end of the Cold War, remains for military applications. In describing how Long Island bridges kept the, largely non-white, poor away from the beaches there, Winner demonstrated how the design of technologies usually favours some ruling group, clique or class over others (Winner, 1986). Habermas further suggests that the technological values of society are largely those of domination. Domination has thus become part and parcel of the rationality of today. In particular, we have become dominated by the principles of growth and technological progress. Such principles, which lead to financial reward for many, provide the basis of the viability and acceptance of this system of control.

Quoting Marcuse, Habermas suggests this domination is the direct symptom of the instantiation of the scientific method. This method, in exercising increasing control over the formerly unruly 'nature', eventually provided the system for the domination of humans by other humans. Scientific innovation is no longer something one analyses and assesses within a democratic rationality to determine best interests. It is now a dogma in that the legitimacy of its dominance is beyond questioning by the average person who is reduced to merely selecting which of its various products to consume. Effectiveness has become more than simply itself in that it is threatening to become the only language for discussion about the world around us. Thus, the successful (or otherwise) introduction of scientific discovery can be measured in this language but the objects themselves cannot. Such discussion either does not take place or is curtailed by the 'inevitability' of science. Weapons of enormous destruction, for example, become not objects for rational discussion but rather items to be measured for their effectiveness in destructive powers or in procuring financial reward. Technocratic principles of effectiveness thus provide the basis for the rationalisation of the 'unfreedom' of man (Habermas, 1971).

In summary, 'the Computer Age' is of extremely loose definition. This fuzziness (a word used in a positive sense by many in the technological field) permits the promotion of fantastical visions of the future. Such visions do not withstand scrutiny in that they are either many centuries away or just plain naïve. These visions of the future, by positing an inevitably brighter world, are part of a wider ethos that attempts to hide real ends. Technology is the most powerful weapon for delivering these ends which are quintessentially dominative in that they attempt to curtail any discussion of themselves. Consequently the computer age is simply symptomatic of a closing down of genuinely democratic practice. The real cause is the technocratic values of effectiveness that limit discussion. Where there should be a rational discussion that engages with technology as to-be-used there is the definitive dogma of futuristic computer age rhetoric.

2.   A Virtual Crisis: The University Mission

Evidence for a university in crisis is not difficult to find. Departments whose sole purpose is to make money (or to be a "cash cow" as the London Business School Director remarked) are a surface indication of a questionable university ethic. Accumulation within the university seems to be a developing theme. Even Cambridge University, despite its enormous wealth, has grabbed funds from Microsoft for a research centre that will inevitably narrow perspectives because some staff will inevitably be involved in one way or another in work that is principally the concern of that giant corporation. Students will imbibe an atmosphere that is less open than it would be otherwise. Management often reinforce this with statements that indicate an amoral view of financial aid. There is a consequent concern that the university mission currently being realised is too blatantly capitalist.

A cursory examination of the literature of the contemporary university crisis would suggest this is a matter of considerable choice. For some, the crisis is fundamentally related to the levels of independence from government intervention and control. However, even these writers seem unable to agree. Both Tooley and Hague for example support a complete severance from all Government control (Tooley, 1996; Hague, 1991). Students should pay their own fees and universities should be allowed to operate in a free market. Writers such as Owen and more recently Sir Ron Dearing support a much more interventionist stance with government policy playing a large determining factor in the direction and mission the university adopts (Owen, 1979; Dearing, 1997). Other writers take issue with the levels of funding available to the university. However, issues such as funding and intervention - issues termed 'functional' by Scott - are not the concern of this chapter (Scott, 1984).

My concern is whether the mission of the university is now bankrupt. Has the university reached, or is it approaching, a point at which a mission within a narrative tradition is no longer tenable? Do conditions exists that predicate a university of discontinuity of mission? Should we rethink the university totally and, if so, what form should this take? Should the university become like a bank or a monastery or should it simply go away?

To many writers the answer is that such predicates do exist. They posit various causes for why this is this is the case and I have listed and discussed the majority of them elsewhere (Preston, 2001). There are many vehicles for these changes to impact upon today's university and it is one these, technology, that I investigate here.

3.   The Virtual University

We have become more dependent on machinery and technology in our daily lives. Robert Pepperell suggests that human beings are no longer seen as independent from the technology around them but are intertwined as one (Pepperell, 1995). Pepperell terms this the 'post-human' condition. When one considers the extent to which we are dependent on, say, the telephone, the concept has a certain resonance in the world we all live in. Technology has become increasingly visible and complex (Bynum and Moor, 1998). In particular the growth in use of ICT can be seen in any hospital, library, high street or home.

The extent to which an individual life engages with technology is relative (Brown, 1996). The unemployed former collier will, in all probability, have much less interaction with ICT. than will a City trader of Futures. I am dealing then in generalisations when I write of the extent to which the university is challenged by ICT. This is compounded by the apparent fact that the forms of ICT I write of here will, in all likelihood, be superseded by the results of ideas as yet unformulated. Nevertheless, these generalisations offer some insight into the type of challenge facing the university.

A fairly common vision of the type of challenge offered to the university mission by ICT is a rather fuzzy hybrid of artificial intelligence, large databases, multimedia and speech-recognition (Harris, 1988). As the argument runs, an Edinburgh University student working at a terminal in Bangkok is able to interact with our conceptual ICT hybrid to learn about her chosen topic. The student can interact with this hybrid via a keyboard, a touch screen or speech-filter. The information about her chosen topic will be held on the database with super-fast software search engines to locate and retrieve sought-after material. Artificial intelligence will determine what and why the student does not fully understand about the topic in question and will respond accordingly. In addition, rather than sit at the back of a stuffy lecture room with poor acoustics where the student attempts to decipher what is being presented, the multimedia system provides high quality sound and vision with unlimited replays of the material. The required distribution of the system in this vision is provided by an amalgamation of communication networks, such as an improved Internet, satellite and optical fibre links. The distribution is handled by a host of accompanying software and is thus transparent to the student. In other words, once this sophisticated infrastructure is put in place, students have few problems setting up and maintaining their learning environment at home or wherever they feel suits them best. The site of learning could of course be mobile. Interaction with the learning environment can take place for an hour during lunch at work, for three hours in the evening at home or even during a long train journey via mobile phone and laptop. University students thus have no travel costs to a geographically fixed university and do not have to compete with other students for books or chairs in the library. In addition, given that the system is available 24 hours a day, the night owl or vacation student is not discriminated against.

Part of the appeal of such a learning structure is the flexibility demonstrated by the Edinburgh student described above (Schlove, 1995). The freedom to choose the when, how and what of learning is in the hands of the student and not the academic staff member. The modern British university mission has demonstrated few of these considerations for the student. In fact it is remarkable how students are generally ignored whenever university missions are discussed (Habermas, 1986). Learning systems are also seen as constantly changing and testimony to this can be found in the dynamism of the accompanying terminology. The etymologically astute have dismissed the term 'distance learning' in asking 'Distance from what?'. 'Virtual university' is a less easily dismissed term and is the one I prefer because the physical presence of bricks and mortar has, since the medieval outset of the university, been fundamental to its mission (Oakeshott, 1949) and the lack of this physical form is the crucial distinguishing feature of the virtual university. The students may be distant from each other or they may not but the ultimate realisation of our dream is a system where no physical body called the university exists. Although *distance* is not an important concept in the language of ICT-driven higher learning it is clear that the geographical outreach of such systems is fundamental to their appeal. In a new economic order such systems, no longer sated on local or national needs, have become global (Kantor, 1995). Modern ICT enables learning to take place concurrently across the whole world (Leebaert, 1999). Unsurprisingly, the British universities have recognised this as an opportunity for expansion without necessarily incurring the costs commensurate with the necessary increases in expensive full-time academic staff (Scott, 1998).

I have outlined the type of system that I believe forms at least part of the reasoning behind any talk of a technologically-inspired university crisis. As I have already suggested, this vision is currently both illusory and unrealisable. Such systems do not exist and are unattainable for the foreseeable future. Part of the reason for this is technological. The rate at which data or images are pumped into our homes and offices via computer networks is too slow, without using inordinately expensive equipment, to provide in real-time either consistently high-quality sound or acceptable levels of visual quality. This is the so-called 'bandwidth problem'. Some writers have suggested that this lack of cyber-power is the only reason that the physical university is still with us (Negroponte, 1996). Even at a technological level, this seems rather naïve or overly optimistic - surely the more difficult problems lie in authentication, security and identity. How will one ensure that a student is who they claim they are? How will one ensure that the system will not result in a university that most suits the computer hacker? There are additional questions over the suitability of virtual (human) interactions. The three-dimensional body has an aura which even a computer-generated hologram does not. The presence in the same room of a dozen of the most sophisticated computers does not register with the human central nervous system at all. It is a fairly obvious remark that computer-generated pictures of one's children far away does not assuage the desire to meet them. I would suggest that the need to sit with other students and with academic mentors is equally vital to learning. Those who deny this may just, through some torpor that is a reversal of the perceived transformation of robot to man, have forgotten what it is to be human.

Although many technological issues remain far from resolved, the greater conceptual difficulties lie in the area of learning itself. Which forms of learning are possible through such systems and which are not? What is the value of the teacher-student communication and how much of this is deliverable through technology? What role does the learner community play in empowering students and how much of this is realisable virtually? These are all difficult questions to which there are few clear answers. However, I will attempt, through example, to demonstrate some of the problems.

Several virtual universities exist across the world. I have examined one of these in some detail and from two perspectives, those of the students and the tutors. The very first virtual university was the National Technological University (NTU), which gained university status in 1984. Although originally offering a strictly engineering and technical programme of courses, NTU now offers a wide range of courses, including philosophy and many languages. In part, NTU operates in a similar vein to the Open University, with regular TV broadcasts, but is dissimilar in that much of the material taught is delivered through computer-mediated and often interactive learning.

I questioned by email several NTU students, who had taken courses from their desks and homes at NTU during the 1997/8 academic year. Although most had enjoyed their experience, many thought they had missed something fundamental to a non-virtual university. The lack of human interaction with fellow students and academics, the necessarily technological interface to learning and the constantly distorted pedagogy were just some of their concerns. I interviewed via phone some of the teaching staff, all of whom were in their first year of involvement, during the same academic year. These staff members were generally extremely satisfied with the experience. However, a large minority of the staff did express some concern that there was a potential problem of students falsifying their identities.

I consider the above example to be evidence of creeping 'micro-technological' concerns within the university. This demonstrates technology being increasingly considered for use in the day-to-day running of the organisation. However, more fundamental to any discourse of university crisis is the 'macro-technological' issue. By this I mean an increased alacrity to use technological values to determine the university mission and future (Bynum and Moor, 1998). Such values are manifest in the contemporary university in: the language of efficiency, utility, inputs, outputs and projects; the dominance of the mass over the individual; the rise of so-called 'spreadsheet economics'; and the rejection of an alternative language of tutelage, efficacy and students (Peters, 1994).

I made a study in some detail of two universities in London. I attended many meetings at various levels and read much of the literature of both institutions and I found macro-technological language to be both commonplace and dominant. The mission statements make projections in terms of percentage growth and coverage. Academic staff seemed acutely aware of the financial implications of a range of possible paths. At one point, during a Board to ratify exam marks, a lecturer highlighted potential disparity in respective treatment between a particular student and others. A Dean remarked that he wasn't prepared to waste time on the grades of any particular student. In a clear attempt to make a claim to objectivity, he suggested we would all be better off for studying the sheet of marks presented to us. I would suggest that, contrary to some opinion, the values of the university today are as technological as most private sector companies. Certainly my observations of almost total macro-technological consideration of university decisions, rather than a more holistic approach, suggest that these no longer align with recent British thought on the philosophy of technology (Bynum and Moor, 1998). This tradition, unlike its American counterpart, is one that reflects on the type of technology that suits our lives rather than how we can best adapt to fit around it: efficacy over efficiency (Negroponte, 1996).

It seems apparent that the university cannot ignore recent technological and scientific developments (Scott, 1995). Technology challenges the university at both micro and macro levels. The former is apparent in the visibility of technological products, although this is not as complete within the university as some perhaps believe. The latter, the use of technological values to drive educational process is more fundamental in that it represents a model for the way decisions are made within the university. Some even claim that the university, in failing to instil these very technological values is in crisis (Hague, 1991). It would seem more reasonable to suggest that the topic of the extent to which the university mission is driven by technological values is one for discussion by the academic and wider communities. Habermas makes clear his concerns that technological systems, in the hands of those who generally control them, are a threat to wider argument in that they restrict the visibility of alternative vistas (Habermas, 1971). Any reluctance to accept these technological values need not be evidence for a discourse of crisis but rather a sign of serious engagement with a question of philosophical importance.

The question inevitably arises as to what might threaten the university. If the university is dispensed with, what might the replacement look like? Or rather, what sort of university-like education might be preferable? Certainly, the university does not hold the monopoly in higher education it once commanded earlier this century (Scott, 1984). For example, the corporate research centre is one, if only partial, alternative. A more radical suggestion is to replace universities with cyber-communities (Sardar and Ravetz, 1996). Such communities already exist in parts of the United States and draft plans have been tabled for one in Sussex, England. These essentially consist of a gated and closed physical environment where like-minded individuals live and work. Such communities are technological superstructures, offering the resident unparalleled speed of access to information. Training, education and many intellectual leisure pursuits, for both parents and children, would be provided by distributed software and hardware systems, similar to those discussed above. Within a futuristic vision such as this, it is not regarded as significant that the knowledge worker may never leave home but rather that she will be unable to differentiate between home and work.

Of course there are many problems with such cyber-communities, including those of purely technical viability and lack of physical propinquity discussed earlier. On a practical level there is little sign of agreement about the actual economics of such systems. More fundamentally, there are concerns about their divisive nature, furthering the divide between the technological 'haves' and 'have-nots' (Winner, 1992).

Nevertheless, with an exponentially increasing speed of technological change, such visions are not lightly disregarded when positing the future mission of the university. Any proposed vision of the university of the future must be cognisant of cyber-communities in order to ensure that the vision provides a preferable solution.

4.   A Profound Crisis

My own view on the crisis of the university is thus quite simple. The rabid accumulating principles of capitalism, or 'turbo-capitalism' as Luttwak has termed it, have created a new breed of capitalists who see the advantage in promulgating the inevitability of change and progress (Luttwak, 1998). The university stands in the way of the capitalist forces seeking advanced financial gains and is thus a potential threat. For centuries, the university has been an active institution of independent opinion and outspokenness, often renouncing the apparently inevitable projected changes to the world. Furthermore, the university has been a place where a multiplicity of distinct perspectives has been argued, often at times against a dangerously suffocating established orthodoxy (Preston, 2001).

By establishing an apparent objective certainty in the form of numeric 'quality' targets, managerialism has successfully concealed its accumulative ends. It makes a bold insurgent attack on alternative perspectives by attempting to make scientific-based discovery congruent with the inevitability of change. Effectiveness, the achievement of the concealed accumulative ends, aggressively tries to become the *lingua franca* of human engagement and judgement. It attempts to destroy alternative forms of measurement. The ethic will attempt to effectively vanquish other perspectives that do not effectively accumulate.

The university has yet to have its mind closed by the new forces of accumulating captialism. News of the demise of the university is premature and there is still time for the university to become a significant voice in the stand against such one-dimensional (that is, efficient) knowledge frameworks. It stands at the critical crossroads between the immoral earnings of turbo-capitalism and the financial impoverishment of moral responsibility.

There is no shortage of critics of such a techno-scientific ethic but the system remains intact. Habermas suggests that by replacing a life-world formed by the rationalisation of science through the discourse of an interacting engaged populace with one that uses scientific 'fact' as that discourse agent we are looking at something more sinister (Habermas, 1971). For this techno-rationalist system of managerialism threatens to eradicate all other alternative methods of forming and perceiving the life-world. Managerialism serves concealed accumulative ends through projecting a subjectively selected set of objectively measured quality criteria. Any doubt about, say, the necessity of constant change is thus effectively proven as invalid. The consequences of strategic progress and change become immaterial in this ethic. Equally, individuals who act on managerialist doctrines with often devastating effects on millions of lives become blame-free. Effectiveness becomes congruent with moral action.

Managerialism effectively measures objectively measured quality indicators and presents these as the life-world itself. Auditing confirms that managerialism is working effectively. The system tries to close all other interpretations of the life-world by reducing existence to a quality-measured space. Suggested alternative paradigms, such as those that question the inevitability of change, must be justified against this dominant ethic of effectiveness. One must not question the destructive tendencies, inhumanity or injustice of the life-world but examine the effective measurement that these supposedly represent. The manager thus has a vital role in modern society. The manager is responsible for ensuring the life-world runs effectively. Given the lofty position of effectiveness, this equates with what used to be known as morality. Replacing morality is the auditing of turbo-capitalist quality flags.

The university, as a late-coming proselyte of the ethic of effectiveness, has taken to it with a great passion. The university is increasingly willing to proclaim the positive side of managerialism, whatever evidence exists in support of the contrary side. Though far from fully established in the university, scientific and technological values have become central to its identity and managerialist discourse is now *de rigeour* (di Norcia, 1994). Newman's warning of science claiming to change a world that it cannot understand has, despite supportive evidence of this happening in the life-world, gone unheeded in today's university (Newman, 1982).

The university is in danger of effectively producing graduates, research and other outputs without ever justifying its actions. The university is an increasingly effective institution. There is little room for, or interest shown in, Aristotelian 'good' or more efficacious or softer forms of assessing the life-world (White, 1990). The university is becoming a strategically-empowered and goal-driven institution (Salter and Tapper, 1992). Turbo-capitalist ends are ever more effectively hidden behind both university brand name marketing and the manicured decency of Armani-clad ex-academic nouveau strategists. Underneath this, upholding the very structure of the university itself, is a foundation of an increasingly techno-rationalist ethos. Ends deeply buried, the university is more and more concerned only with means. The question that is continually asked in the contemporary university is 'How?' whilst 'Why?' is seldom asked.

Habermas suggests that contemporary techno-scientific rationality has ambitions of ultimately closing down all other paradigms (Habermas, 1971). Increasingly beset by this rationality, it would seem clear that the perceived crisis of the university is in essence a moral one. Modern morality must be efficient. A techno-scientific ethic is replacing morality with effectiveness within the university.

The university seems to have the ambition of becoming one cog, indistinguishable from all the others, within a machine dominated by the combined values of technology and market economics (Ryder, 1996; Derrida, 1983). Elliot even suggests that successive governments and other bodies have for so long treated the university as a machine or factory that the university has accordingly responded as one (Elliot, 1999). Yesterday's students have become today's customers (Scott, 1997).

Macmurray's remark that the economic exists purely to serve the personal is thus reversed within the ethic of effectiveness (Macmurray, 1961). The other side of the coin of this university ethic becomes the disregard of the contemplative and the subjective (Barnett, 1997a). The objective has become transformed into dogma. X may have fundamentally different views from Y but the ethic insists a resolution be found. X must beat Y or Y must beat X. A winner must always be found in this conflict. The assumption that the inherent conflict between any rationally motivated parties is always reconcilable is more than questionable. Within this discourse of effectiveness the university plays a vital but limited role in this conflict resolution. Morals must be handed on through instruction as skills (Blake, 1998). The 'given' that moral conflict is always resolvable runs counter to my analysis of this chapter and elsewhere (Preston, 2001). Certainly in imposing such a dictum the ethic constrains the university. The assumption of conflict resolution becomes unquestionable. Other issues of dubious authenticity are equally ring-fenced as objective truth. This limitation of what and how topics can be discussed is indicative of the ethic having had some success in its aim of excluding alternative voices. Managerialism, effectiveness, strategy and technology have become, despite evidence of their lack of efficacy, extremely important within the university. To question the appropriateness or acceptability of their use is increasingly impermissible within the university. Likewise, the permanence of change has become both established as a doctrine and equated with the value of the university (Tett, 1993). Change in the university has become a desired and prized state.

Surely this impressive list of unchallengeable views is testimony of the moral crisis within the university. If the university will not discuss significant issues, it is no surprise that it has internal structures little different to those of business, industry or government. When the university offered something different to mainstream corporate organisations it was relatively easy to predict a future of positive relationships between the two. However, with the university having adopted values of efficiency similar to those traditional to business and industry it would appear certain that the two identities will soon, at least partially, merge. The university will do business and business will do higher education. The dividing line between the academic and the industrial will inevitably become smudged and later erased (Thompson, 1970). The ethic of effectiveness has dramatically narrowed the scope of the questions the university asks. If the university continues in this vein it will be in danger of becoming an increasingly amoral institution, a 'Diploma Mill' (Noble, 1998).

The university has been since its inception a tremendous force of stability. The medieval university represented a solid and trusted institution resisting a societal drift toward violence. The university in its scholarship was exemplar of a society based on a battle of minds rather than of weapons. Likewise, the 19th Century university fought intellectually against the dominant industrial values, making a case for something both more human and historically suited to the cultural situation. For the university to suddenly renege on this role of engaging with and influencing the dynamic forces of society may harbour untold dangers and for the university to suddenly become totally at the beck and call of combined societal forces would be a further demonstration of a rationality having had successfully eliminated alternative voices.

The obvious question is what form should the university aspire to in the 21st Century and beyond. Certainly, surrounding society need not have a direct effect on the university or vice versa. The effects of the Industrial Revolution were severely attenuated in comparison with the effects on society. Similarly, the medieval university was in turmoil over re-discovered Greek and Roman texts but this made few corresponding ripples in the world outside (Preston, 2001). Any analysis that equates the respective changes within societal and university as functionally dependent is in itself taking a disputable position. We cannot take as read that what changes one must alter the other.

5.   Knowledge Frameworks and a University of Moral Enquiry
If the university continues to follow its current trajectory towards a totally techno-scientific rationality, it will soon lose all recognition as a source of vistas alternative to that of dominant managerialism. It will become another part of the machine of accumulative turbo-capitalism. Any claims of it providing an alternative and significant voice in society will be invalid.

Britain has a long tradition as a service sector economy (Rubinstein, 1993). As such, knowledge replaces physical labour as the most significant commodity of exchange (Smith and Scase, 1997). Hence the university, whose 'goods' have always been strongly associated with knowledge, has a vital role within the British economy (Dearing, 1997). The university has awoken to both the power and the financial value of knowledge (Borgmann, 1999). Managerialism seems to have fully accepted that knowledge has finally become power within the university

(Lyotard, 1984). Ideas have increasingly become a commodity and the university has become a capitalist industry (Tett, 1993). A part of a larger monopolistic information market (Melody, 1997). The university seems intent on promoting the commodification of knowledge and this finds approval within society at large (Lawrence, 1999; King, 1983). Wisdom means winning, with the rewards in hard currency. However, such tidy connections are not as inevitable or justifiable as they first appear.

Some ideas defining the mission of the university through knowledge often end up being recursive or self-referential. For example, Scott desires a university mission as a place designed for constructing answers to questions such as 'What is the University mission?' (Scott, 1993). This is both superficially attractive and somewhat limited in that it fails to satisfactorily identify what other similar questions might be. It is a pseudo-recursion in that it provides the starting condition without the onward mapping. Ultimately it says nothing. More reasonably, Alisdair MacIntyre described the university as a place where knowledge can be argued out and accepted positions found (MacIntyre, 1990). MacIntyre seems to be seeking a return to the Scottish Enlightenment, where philosophy was used as the ultimate mechanism in determining accepted and agreed rightful action for an educated public. However, this too is unsatisfactory in that it seems to regard knowledge as a set of canonical texts to be referenced by future generations. The difficulty with this is that it says little of how such texts come about.

Both between and within disciplines there are very different ways of evaluating and analysing knowledge. The economist has one model, the philosopher another, even though their topic (such as technology) may be the same (Liedman, 1997). The ethic of effectiveness within the university, in making claims to objective truth, is threatening to remove this diversity. It compels all alternative paradigms to be measured against its own values. The university today is increasingly more comfortable being 'in method' than 'in truth', as Kierkegaard would put it (Kierkegaard, 1971). Managerialism wishes to straitjacket knowledge paradigms. The effectiveness paradigm has turned into a vengeful taskmaster, seeking to quiet all others (Habermas, 1971; Kuhn, 1962). Such absolute knowledge, obtained through very defined and disciplined means, is increasingly foundational of today's university.

The obvious danger of restricting knowledge within the university to particular market-driven knowledge views is lack of differentiation. It would differ little from alternatives such as corporate research centres. The university surely, for its own welfare, needs wider and more multifarious frames of knowledge than afforded by the discourse of techno-scientific managerialism (Simon, 1994). Indeed, it seems certain to fail to suppress such moral division and will, in all probability, injure itself permanently

(MacIntyre, 1996). In muffling diversity, the university is likely to become a victim of effectiveness itself.

These alternative expanded views of knowledge might just form the very foundation needed to escape the moral crisis within the university. These alternative views of knowledge are crucial to the future vision of the university that I wish to propose since it is through these that the university will differ from all other bodies. My vision of the university is as a place where frameworks for knowledge appraisal are negotiated and agreed through a narrative of tradition. It is unlike MacIntyre's vision in that it is the framework of knowledge rather than the knowledge itself that is agreed upon.

The university should become an institution where the respective structures for considering the life-world are fought over and a place where nothing is assured apart from acceptance of the use of agreed knowledge frameworks. Current frameworks are themselves foundational on other frameworks as they are iterated and changed into those of the future. In introducing students to contemporary and past frameworks, the university initiates minds into the (framework) traditions of thought and enquiry.

No knowledge is 'given' but is subject to the concurrent knowledge frameworks. As important phenomena occur in the life-world they will be evaluated against the existing frameworks. Two differing concurrent frameworks may interpret the phenomena in different ways. Such diverse viewpoints will be then dissected and discussed within the university. The merits and drawbacks of each interpretation will be analysed, producing a deep understanding of the phenomena themselves and how they fits into the whole. Conflict will not thus be crushed, as in the managerial discourse, but resolved by enabling all to see how decisions were made. In addition the same phenomena happening a year later whilst analysed the same way may produce very different outcomes. The use of knowledge frameworks is the only 'given'. Interpretations of the life-world, unlike in managerialism, are not pre-determined.

Research will be formulated through the acceptance and recognition of rival frameworks of enquiry. Students will learn to be flexible intellects, questioning any givens and both asking and answering questions based on diverse frameworks of enquiry. My university mission is thus to be a critic of our culture and an institution of moral enquiry (MacIntyre, 1990; Lipkin, 1994).

John Ladd suggests that it is academic obligation to pronounce on issues that are significant (Ladd, 1970). In the last thirty years this has in practice been vanquished in the university. Fundamental to my university of moral enquiry is knowledge communication. The university must become vocal in its morality. For clarity's sake the university must make these complex ideas transparent through simple language. The enquiry will need to link to both the internal, through teaching, and the external life-world. The exact details of how this can be achieved will need to come through the tradition of knowledge frameworks. However, some ideas I believe might develop from these conversations would be encouragement to integration throughout the university. I suggest that cross-curricular work, by both staff and students, would further knowledge. The greater the diversity of knowledge frameworks known to individuals, the more acceptable is likely to be the ensuing interpretation. In interpreting phenomena a philosopher may use one perspective, a scientist another and the economist a third. By putting the three together in a cross-fertilised interpretation the result is likely to both more profound and satisfactory. Of course there will be much more work involved. Such frameworks will be less efficient, in the short-term at least. However, experiments suggest that more efficacious 'soft' forms of interpreting the world are in the longer-term more efficient. The deeper understanding of phenomena prevents much of the conflict and reversals of managerialism. The ethic of effectiveness expends much time and energy silencing alternative views (Tait, 1999). Having examined the event in the life-world from multifarious viewpoints, knowledge frameworks make largely unnecessary such suffocation of opinion. Indeed, the frameworks are based on the principle of encouraging broad-based opinions rather than domination of them. In addition, it would seem likely that the frameworks would both diminish ignorance and foster tolerance (Damrosch, 1995).

Disagreement and conflict are inevitable in my reading of the post-Enlightenment world. Analysis of evidence through the traditional knowledge frameworks is my recommended route to reach an acceptable compromise in how right action is identified. This is distinct from a victory or conclusion. In all probability, neither side will 'win' but a moral understanding is the aim (Young, 1989). It is a morality constructed in the diversity of knowledge rather than pure economics or the constraints of some managerialist rack (Hoskin, 1998).

There have always been powerful forces in society that, whilst claiming a perspective of disinterest, harbour a desire to radically alter the world to their own ends. In utilising my diverse knowledge frameworks the university will return to its historic and vital role in resisting such forces. In particular, managerialism and its accompanying techno-scientific ethic of effectiveness would themselves be subject to open discussion. Even the accumulative ends that have overtaken modern Britain and are surfacing within the university would need to be analysed in the harsh light of this normative contemporary knowledge framework.

As mentioned above, it is my view that if the university continues on its path toward a 'hard' strategic managerialism it will be entering very murky waters. The danger signs are already there. The university seems to care less and less about its image of a certain independence from the turbo-capitalist world. Likewise, national newspaper stories (The Guardian 1st

November 1999) of wide pay disparity between male and female academic staff hint at inequality within the university. The university has recently deflected such criticism by suggesting it is an old dog trying to learn new tricks (Mohrman, 1994). How long the university can maintain its pretence of a quaint naïveté is questionable.

The university is at risk of causing a wider body of people to distrust it intensely. Whilst making claims of being democratic, the results have been at best disappointing (Weinstein, 1991). By adopting an increasingly managerialist position the university is at risk of appearing as an accommodating host to institutional racism, sexism and class discrimination (Wallace, 1999). I do not believe that currently such accusations have substance. It is more likely that the university, in trying to adopt an ethic of effectiveness, makes rash decisions whose outcomes appear to hide more sinister ambitions (Snook, 1995). However, in time action tends to negate intent. If the university continues for much longer in this vein of pragmatic effective decision-making it will amount to an institution that renounces any claims of independent interpretation of the life-world.

Implicit in my knowledge frameworks above is democracy. In order to create an atmosphere conducive to moral enquiry all must be free to speak. University education should be a broad-based moral debate carried out through a tradition of accepted knowledge frameworks. As a result of this conversation the frameworks for future knowledge are iterated and decided. It is thus fundamentally democratic. To deny X a voice will restrict the validity and acceptability of the interpretations made (Dewey, 1937). Democracy requires that any question can be asked and that each be treated equally within the tradition. My belief is that my university of moral enquiry will need to be democratic.

Max Scheler, often nicknamed 'the Catholic Nietzsche', produced a highly moral philosophy but led a dissolute life. When asked how he squared these two facets of his existence Scheler replied, "Whoever heard of a signpost going the way of its signing?" (Frings, 1997). Today's university is neither democratic signpost nor hiker seeking democracy. It neither preaches nor practices democracy. Under the control of a strategic rudder, democracy and the university increasingly resemble opposites, a situation Beloff suggests is the natural order (Beloff, 1975). But the university needs to be democratic to avoid a narrowly restricted interpretation of the life-world (Derrida, 1983). To reuse Scheler's metaphor, I believe that university should become a signpost that all can read, representative of and toward democracy.

During the last hundred years or so the university has demonstrated almost total disregard for the educated public community it purports to serve (Barnett, 1997b). Any erstwhile ethic of social responsibility has totally disappeared (Nemerowitz and Rosi, 1997). The academic's human network increasingly contains a disparate list of parties including many concerned only with financial reward and efficiency. In addition, the university often goes to great lengths to form these links, seeking them in far-flung corners of the world. In becoming increasingly concerned for the financial, the university, often with unwitting support from the government through favourable funding policies, frequently seeks ties with exotic locations on the other side of the world rather than with the educated public of their own backyard. Schlove even suggests that the lack of community-based research is symptomatic of the university crisis of mission (Schlove, 1998).

Many examples of this disregard for the university's community are readily available. Indeed, this is part of a wider phenomenon that demonstrates how little the university learns about itself and its community (Barnett, 1997a). Often truly significant developments within the community are totally ignored by the university (Melody, 1997). This failure to engage with such issues as they form and develop has resulted in the university being seen as part of economic rather than social policy (Neave, 1988).

There is much evidence that the British university is in a moral crisis. Essentially it spends most of its time both asking and answering questions in very restricted ways. The exclusion of certain vistas is enforced and included paradigms are managed by the prevailing mechanisms of the ethic of effectiveness. My argument has been that the desired state for the university is one of moral enquiry. Contrary to obvious perceptions, this does not amount to the same thing as the recent transparency of ethics, as demonstrated by the prevalence of Codes of Conduct for example, within the university. My argument is that such a university will need to be built on diverse iterative knowledge frameworks. Such framing will also need to be based on open recognition of a narrative of tradition and indeed a university of moral enquiry would become the place where knowledge frameworks are discussed and verified. If a new framework becomes accepted then it, in turn, forms part of the tradition itself. I have also argued that the university will require a radical transformation into a democratic and communicative institution. Democracy implies a community. The university will need to become bound bi-directionally to its community of an educated public.

A university of moral enquiry based in and fostering a democratic community is ambition beyond ambition since if my reading of the inevitability of post-Enlightenment conflict is correct, the university of moral enquiry is unlikely to succeed against the instantiation of managerial values and ideals. Nevertheless such ambition is in itself both admirable and meritorious. Like Max Scheler, the university will probably fall short of its own pronounced values. Søren Kierkegaard suggests a life of failing ambition is infinitely preferable to an ambition of failure (Kierkegaard,

1971). It is to be hoped that this chapter demonstrates that a Democratic University of Moral Enquiry that does not live up to its own aims is fvastly preferable to the currently strategically correct but immoral university.

6.   Conclusions

Many questions concerning technology remain unanswered and too frequently unasked. Current levels of computer sophistication are far outstripped by the claims made for such technologies. Impressive advances has been made in improving the efficiency of technological systems while obvious questions of efficacy remain untouched. We frequently mass produce automata that would have been better left on a designer's experimental workbench. Furthermore, despite claims of a technologically-inspired globalised awareness, ideological change, unlike the lower forms of social and conceptual realignments, remains both easy to talk up and equally difficult to find.

My research indicates that the commonly perceived contemporary university 'crisis' is the result of neither technology nor work practices. It is rather primarily attributable to the establishment of strategic managerialism, with its underlying ethic of effectiveness, as the dominant discourse. This in turn can be traced back to the fallout from the ideological shift of the Enlightenment. Managerialism and the voice of effectiveness are the results of paradoxes thrown up by an objective scientific world. Once the neutrality of science became subject to apparent dispute a dominant mechanism of resolving conflict needed to be found in order to hide and protect accumulative ends. This techno-scientific ethic of effectiveness has been instantiated in the UK. As Habermas suggests, it is an ethic that ultimately aims to close down all alternative paradigms. With its ambition of dominating the way the life-world is perceived, managerialism and the ethic of effectiveness is an obvious threat to the mission of the modern university.

My vision for the future of the university mission is one of moral enquiry. Such enquiry will necessarily be both communicated and open, with no forbidden questions. It will be based in a knowledge framework of tradition, a tradition that is currently in a phase of post-Enlightenment diversity. It will require, and is required by, democracy. The university will thus speak clearly and morally from the enquiry it carries out. The post-Enlightenment condition ensures that there will be many disappointments and failures ahead. However, the alternatives are most likely to manufacture and accelerate the very crises that many contemporary voices claim to forewarn.

References

Barnett, R. (1997a), *Realising the university*. London: London University.

Barnett, R. (1997b), *Higher Education: A Critical Business*. Buckingham: The Society for the Research into Higher Education.

Bell, D. (1962), *The End of Ideology: on the exhaustion of political ideas in the fifties*. Collier.

Beloff, M. (1975), *Can the universities survive?* in: (Box, 1975): 45-50.

Blake, N., Smith, R. and Standish, P. (1998), *The universities we need* London: Kogan Page.
Brown, W.S. (1996), 'Technology, workplace privacy and personhood', *Journal of business ethics* 15: 1237-1248.

Borgmann, A. (1999), *Holding on to reality: The nature of information at the turn of the Millennium*. Chicago: University of Chicago.

Brzezinski, Z.K. (1976), *Between two ages: America's role in the technetronic era*. Viking Press.

Bynum, T.W. and Moor, J. (eds.) (1998), *The digital Phoenix: How computers are changing philosophy*. Blackwell.

Damrosch, D. (1995), *We scholars: Changing the culture of the university*. Cambridge, MA: Harvard University Press.

Dearing, R. (1997), *Higher education in the learning society*. Norwich: Crown Publications.

Derrida, J. (1983), 'The principle of reason: The university in the eyes of its pupils', *Diacritics*. Fall 1983: 3-20.

Dewey, J. (1937*)*, 'Democracy and educational administration', *School and society,* 45(1):162-178.

di Norcia, V. (1994), 'Ethics, technology development and innovation', *Business Ethics Quarterly*. 4(3): 235-252.

Elliot, L. (1999), 'Still stuck in the machine age groove', *The Guardian*. April 21 1999.

Frings, M.S. (1997), *The Mind of Max Scheler*. Fordham University Press.

Habermas, J. (1971), *Towards a rational society*. London: Heinemann.

Habermas, J. (1975), *Legitimation Crisis*. Heinemann Educational.

Habermas, J. (1986), *The idea of the university: Learning process*. Heidelberg: University of Heidelberg.

Hague, D. (1991), 'Beyond universities: A new republic of the intellect', London: Institute of Economic Affairs (Hobart Paper 115).

Harris, D. (ed.) (1988), *Education for the new technologies*. London: Kogan Page.

Harvey, D. (1989), *The condition of postmodernity*. Oxford: Basil Blackwell.

Hoskin, K. (1998), 'Examining accounts and accounting for management: Inverting understandings of 'the economic', (McKinlay and Starkey, 1998): Chapter 6.

Kantor, R.M. (1995), *World class: Thriving locally in the global economy* New York: Touchstone.

Kierkegaard, S. (1971), *Either/Or Vol. 1 and 2*. New Jersey: Princeton University Press.

King, D.W. (ed.) (1983), *Key papers in the economics of information*. New York: Greenwood Publishing Group.

Kuhn, T.S. (1962), *The structure of scientific revolutions*. Chicago: The University of Chicago Press.

Ladd, J. (1970), 'Morality and the ideal of rationality in formal organisations', *The Monist*. 54: 488-516.

Lawrence, D. (1999), *Economic value of information*. Chicago: University of Chicago.

Leebaert, D. (ed.) (1999), *The future of the electronic marketplace*. Boston, MA: MIT.

Liedman, S-E. (ed.) (1997), The postmodernist critique of the project of Enlightenment. Atlanta, GA: Rodolphi.

Lipkin, R.J. (1994), 'Pragmatism, cultural criticism and the idea of the postmodern university', in:. (Sellars, 1994): 49-88.

Luttwak, E.L. (1998), *Turbo Capitalism.* London: Wiedenfield and Nicolson.

Lyotard, J-F. (1984), *The postmodern condition: A report on knowledge.* Manchester: Manchester University Press.

MacIntyre, A. (1990), *Three rival versions of moral enquiry.* London: Duckworth.

MacIntyre, A. (1996), *Whose Justice? Which Rationality?* 2*nd* *Edition* London: Duckworth.

Macmurray, J. (1961), *Persons in relation.*London: Faber.

McKinlay, A. and Starkey, K. (eds.) (1998), *Foucault, management and organisation theory.* London: Sage.

Melody, W. (1997), 'Universities and public policy', in: (Smith and Webster, 1997): 72-84.

Mohrman, K. (1994), 'Ethical implications of curricular reform', in: (Sellars, 1994): 117-126.

Moor, J. (1990), 'Ethics of privacy protection', *Library Trends,* 39(1) and 39(2): 69-82.

Neave, G. (1988), 'Education and social policy: Demise of an ethic or a change of values', *Oxford review of education.* 14(3): 273-283.

Negroponte, N. (1996), *Being Digital.* New York: Vintage Books.

Nemerowitz, G. and Rosi, E. (1997), *Education for leadership and social responsibility.* London: The Falmer Press.

Newman, J.H. (1982), *The idea of a university.* University of Notre Dame Press.

Noble, D. (1998),'Digital diploma mills', *Technological knowledge review.* 1(1).

Oakeshott, M. (1949), 'The universities', *The Cambridge Journal,* 2: 515-42.

Orwell, G. (1998), *1984.* Penguin Books.

Owen, T.A. (1979), *The relationship between society and university institutions in Great Britain.* University of Wales MA Thesis.

Pepperell, R. (1995), *The post-human condition.* Exeter: Intellect Books.

Peters, M. (1994), 'Performance, the future of the university and post-industrial society', *Educational philosophy and theory.* 26(1): 1-22.

Piore, M. and Sabel, C. (1984), *The second industrial divide.* New York: Scholastic.

Preston, D.S. (2001), '*Technology, managerialism and the university.* Fife, Scotland: Glenrothes Publications.

Rubinstein, W.D. (1993), *Capitalism, culture and decline in Britain 1750-1990.* London: Routledge.

Ryder, A. (1996), 'Reform and UK higher education in the enterprise era', *Higher education quarterly.* 50(1): 54-70.

Salter, B. and Tapper, T. (1992), *Oxford, Cambridge and the changing idea of the university: the challenge to donnish domination*, Buckingham: Society for Research into Higher Education: Open University Press.

Sardar, Z. and Ravetz, J.R. (eds.) (1996), *Cyberfutures: culture and politics on the information superhighway.* London: Pluto.

Schlove, R.E. (1995), *Democracy and technology.* New York: The Guildford Press.

Schlove, R.E. (1998), 'The democratic uses of technology', *Thought and Action.* 14(1).

Scott, P. (1984), *The crisis of the university.* Sydney: Croom Helm

Scott, P. (1993), 'The idea of the university in the 21st Century: A British perspective', *British journal of educational studies.* 1: 14-25.

Scott, P. (1995), *The meaning of mass higher education.* Buckingham: Open University.

Scott, P. (1997), 'The postmodern university', in: (Smith and Webster, 1997): 36-47.

Scott, P. (ed.) (1998), *The globalisation of higher education.* Buckingham: Open University.

Sellars, M.N.S. (ed.) (1994), *An ethical university.* Oxford: Berg.

Simon, R.L. (1994), 'Neutrality, politicization and the curriculum', in: (Sellars, 1994): 89-106.

Smith, A. and Webster, F. (eds.) (1997), *The postmodern university? Contested visions of higher education in society.* Buckingham: The Society for Research into Higher Education: Open University.

Smith, A. and Scase R. (1997), 'Conclusion: An affirming flame', in (Smith and Webster, 1997): 99-113.

Snook, I. (1995), 'Democracy and education in a monetarist society', *Educational philosophy and theory.* 27(1): 55-68.

Tait, J. (1999), 'Help for the academic nomads in search of their own sympathetic tribe', *The Times Higher Education Supplement* 5th March 1999.

Tett, L. (1993), 'Education and the marketplace', *Scottish Educational Review,* 25(2):121-131.

Thompson, E.P. (ed.) (1970), *Warwick University Ltd: Industry Management and the Universities.* Harmondsworth: Penguin Books.

Toffler, A. (1980), *The third wave.* New York: William Morrow and Company.

Tooley, J. (1996), *Education without the State.* London: IEA Education and Training Unit.

Touraine, A. (1974), *The post-industrial society: Tomorrow's social history. Classes, conflicts and culture in the programmed society.* London: Wildwood House.

Wallace, J. (1999) 'The colour blind spot', *The Times Higher Education Supplement* 5th March 1999.

Weinstein, M. (1991), 'Critical thinking and education for democracy', *Educational philosophy and theory*, 23(2): 9-29.

White, J. (1990), *Education and the good life.* London: Kogan Page.

Winner, L. (1986), *The whale and the reactor.* Chicago: Univ. of Chicago Press.
Winner, L. (1992), *Autonomous technology.* Cambridge, MA: The Massachusetts Institute of Technology.

Wittgenstein, L. (1963), *Philosophical investigations.* London: Blackwell.

Young, R.E. (1989), *A critical theory of education.* New York: Harvester Wheatsheaf.

Notes On Contributors

Kate Boardman is a Learning Technologist in the University of Durham IT Service. She has responsibility for duo (Durham University Online), the learning environment that was implemented in October 2000. From studying modern languages she moved to medieval art and literature. She has worked on a number of projects including the digitisation of manuscripts from Durham Cathedral Muniments and an international research project on the Bayeux Tapestry. The latter project draws together scholars from England and France in new research on the textile and Kate has worked on the production of a CD-ROM of the entire Tapestry that includes scrolling images zoomable to individual stitch detail. Kate's PhD thesis is entitled "Origins and influences: The Scandinavian textile context to the Bayeux Tapestry".

Adrian Bromage presently works at Coventry University's Centre for Higher Education Development (CHED) and is involved in two research projects, an evaluation of the University's 'Learn Online' initiative and the ESERC-funded ETL project.

Alan Davis has been Vice President Academic at Athabasca University since 1996 and before that he directed programs at the BC Open University. His original discipline was chemistry, and he received his doctorate from Simon Fraser University in 1980. He has special interests in learning assessment and accreditation, the management of e-learning, and virtual university consortia. In August 2003, he will join Niagara College in Ontario.

Mike Fuller is Senior Lecturer in Econometrics and Social Statistics at the Canterbury Business School of the University of Kent in the United Kingdom. He writes on aspects of ICT and learning, most recently on student project support using ICT. Earlier work focused on ICT in statistics education but also takes in issues of course design and professional development in HE using ICT. He also runs a number of JISCmail lists in the discipline areas of management and of statistics, and also for staff and educational development. His home page is http://www.statistics.fsnet.co.uk/mff.html

Andy Lapham is currently a Principal Lecturer in the London College of Music and Media - a faculty of Thames Valley University, London (TVU) where he is the Pathway Leader of the BA Design for Interactive Media. His expertise lies in the area of HCI and interface design. This extends into teaching web design and other aspects of multimedia computing. His current research considers the design and use of interface metaphors, particularly in relation to virtual learning environments and networked learning.

Brent Muirhead has a BA in social work and Master's degrees in religious education, history, administration, distance education and doctoral degrees in education. He is the area chair for the Master of Arts in education program in curriculum and technology for the University of Phoenix Online where he teaches graduate classes and mentors faculty candidates. He is an Associate Editor for the journal *Educational technology and society*. He is editor of Online Learning and writes a column for the *Journal of the United States Distance Learning Association*.

David Seth Preston has degrees from the universities of London, Loughborough and Sheffield. His background is in applied Information Systems especially within engineering firms. He is author of over a hundred refereed papers and four books.. His interests are in the ethical issues raised by technology. He is married with three children and his main wish for the future is the continued well being of his family. His subsidiary hopes include the development of English universities that are not rife with corruption.

Melissa Lee Price has over twenty years experience in the media industry. She received her doctorate in Higher Education Administration from the University of South Carolina in 1993 where her research focused on the use of different media in distance education. She has continued to research and publish on the use of computer mediated education, as well as producing design award winning instructional material. Dr. Price is a pioneer in the use of synchronous communication in web-based distance education on the university level and has been using the web for online teaching since 1995. She is currently a Reader in Design at Staffordshire University in Stoke on Trent, United Kingdom where she is also the course leader for the Master's Program in Interactive Multimedia at the School of Art and Design. Dr. Price was the first winner of the Broadcast Education Association's Interactive Multimedia Award in 1998. In 2003 she won 'Best of Competition' in the BEA Media Festival's instructional category. Her students' work in educational interactive multimedia has won over fifty international multimedia awards since 1998.

Lynda Ross returned to Athabasca University in 2000 and since then has managed the Educational Media Development Department and is currently Manager of Special Projects with the Office of the Vice President Academic. She has been involved in a variety of institutional research and online course development projects and has authored several open and distance learning courses. Lynda has a doctorate in psychology from the University of New Brunswick and previously held a postdoctoral fellowship tenured at the University of Saskatchewan.

Mark Stiles is Professor of Technology-Supported Learning at Staffordshire University. In his role as Head of Learning Development and Innovation he is charged with leading e-learning across the institution. Staffordshire has been using VLEs for some five years, including the COSE VLE which was developed at Staffordshire and is now available as a free binary/open source product. Mark has led numerous projects relating to the technical, strategic and educational aspects of the use of VLEs/MLEs. He is a regular speaker and has been published widely in these areas. Apart from his current role, Mark's background includes teaching in Further Education and being an IT services manager.

Craig Thomson is an educationalist whose experience straddles a range of sectors, levels and national settings. He has worked in school, further and higher education and has experience as a teacher, manager, teacher trainer and researcher. His experience, in both private and public sector roles, has been gained in Scotland, England and the Middle East. He has also worked in consultancy and project-based roles in Eastern Europe and the United States. He is currently Principal of Glenrothes College, Fife, Scotland. In addition, he is Non-Executive Director of Scottish University for Industry and a member of the Advisory Council of Learning and Teaching Scotland. Craig has degrees from Heriot Watt, Bath and Sheffield Universities. He was the author and co-author of three submissions to the Inquiry into Lifelong Learning conducted recently by the Enterprise and Lifelong Learning Committee of the Scottish Parliament and was invited by the Committee to provide a private in-person briefing during the drafting of their Report.

Mike Waring is a Senior Lecturer in the Department of Sport and Health at the University of Durham. He has been involved in teacher education and higher education for well over ten years, establishing a number of postgraduate and undergraduate courses at different higher education institutions in the UK. The University of Durham acknowledged the quality of his teaching and associated research with the presentation of the University's Excellence in Teaching Award in 2002. He helped to pilot and continues to lead developments in the use of a virtual learning environment at Durham (Durham University Online) around postgraduate and undergraduate physical education and sport courses. One strand of his research involves the critical debate and evaluation of current and future directions and practices in teaching and learning in schools and HEIs with a view to enhancing the learning experiences and critical thinking of trainees and students.

James Wood, Professor and former Chair of Sociology at San Diego State University, is active in three related areas of interests: collective behaviour/social movements; political sociology; and higher education policy. He teaches a graduate seminar combining these interests which focuses on the politics of higher education. He continues his many activities on behalf of higher education for San Diego State University, California, and the U.S., having served as a member of the National Council of the American Association of University Professors (AAUP), as Political Action/Legislative Chair at SDSU and as a member of the parallel state-wide committee for the California Faculty Association (CFA). He has been presented awards from CFA and AAUP for outstanding service to the faculty and higher education. He has published several discussions on higher education funding, distance learning, copyright, tenure and educational quality, and has given many public presentations about higher education. He has won eight Most Influential or Most Outstanding Professor Awards for his teaching in Sociology. His scholarly activities have included writing five books, six monographs, thirty articles and book chapters and the editing of two journals.

Index